IT’S A

JUNGLE

IN THERE

IT'S A JUNGLE IN THERE

INSPIRING LESSONS, HARD-WON INSIGHTS, AND OTHER ACTS OF ENTREPRENEURIAL DARING

SECOND EDITION

STEVEN SCHUSSLER
CREATOR OF RAINFOREST CAFE, T-REX, YAK & YETI, AND THE BOATHOUSE AT WALT DISNEY WORLD®
WITH MARVIN KARLINS

SCHUSSLER
CREATIVE INSTITUTE
GOLDEN VALLEY, MN

Published by
Schussler Creative Institute Publishing
Golden Valley, MN
www.schusslercreative.com

Publisher's Cataloging-in-Publication Data
Schussler, Steven.

It's a jungle in there : inspiring lessons, hard-won insights, and other acts of entrepreneurial daring / Steven Schussler with Marvin Karlins. – 2nd ed. – Golden Valley, MN : Schussler Creative Institute Pub., 2019.

p. ; cm.

ISBN13: 978-0-9980072-0-5

1. Schussler, Steven. 2. Entrepreneurship. 3. Creative ability in business. 4. New business enterprises. I. Title. II. Karlins, Marvin.

HB615.S38 2019
658.421—dc23 2018906281

Project coordination by Jenkins Group, Inc.
www.BookPublishing.com

Layout design by Brooke Camfield

Printed in Malaysia

23 22 21 20 19 • 5 4 3 2 1

To my family and friends who have so boldly shared my vision . . . your selfless devotion, camaraderie, shared passion, and enthusiasm gave me the credibility and wisdom to accept nothing less than yes. I could not have done it without all my friends from the Walt Disney World Company (Bud Dare, Maribeth Bisienere, George Aguel, Joe Rohde, Wing Chao, Keith Bradford, David Stofcik, Scott Benjamin, Jeffrey Abraham, Rachel Alde, Peter Caramalis, Lisa Onopa, Steve Roach, Theron Skees, Jillian DeKunder, Tiffany Rende, George Gross, Robert Iger, Steven Ruffner, Jack Blitch, Joyce Bowers, Michael Colglazier, Jean Marie Clement, Jim MacPhee, Tim Conklin, Ned Waters, Doris Woodward, Jeanette Lomboy, Brent Davies, George Kalogridis, Michele Gendreau, Jessie Chen, Nicolas DeLarocque, and James Gravante), Jimmy Rittenberg, Lyle Berman, Herb Simon, Mel Simon, Tilman Fertitta, Nasser Kazeminy, John Goodman, Doug Holod, Dan Lowe, Steve Graham, Richard Tettamant, Jon Donahue, Brent Kroener, Ken Cooley, Brian Stone, Tim Myslajek, Norm Pink, Dr. Bob Goldman, David Siegel, and Paul Ridgeway.

To my team at Schussler Creative—how lucky I am to have such a talented and dedicated team. My parents, Gloria and Jules; my grandfather, Bill Botwinik; my brothers, Robert and John; and my wife, Sunhi Ryan-Schussler.

To the gatekeepers, hardworking everyday folk, and guests of our restaurants and attractions who shared my dreams, accepted my out-of-the-box thinking, and helped me get where I wanted to go.

CONTENTS

Preface ix

Section I: Personality

Chapter 1: The Role of Risk-Taking in Entrepreneurial Success 3

Chapter 2: The Importance of Passion 15

Chapter 3: Ambition: Taking Your Passions Public 31

Chapter 4: I Dream . . . Therefore I Can 35

Chapter 5: The Multitasker 41

Chapter 6: Layer, Then Layer Some More 47

Section II: Product

Chapter 7: Be Excellent or Be Gone 55

Chapter 8: Sweat the Small Stuff: Paying Attention to Details 59

Chapter 9: Always Be on the Lookout for Your Next Big Thing 65

Chapter 10: Research and Development: Learn It If You Want to Earn It 71

Chapter 11: Make Improvements—Before and After 77

Chapter 12: On Marketing: Customers Won't Buy What They Don't Know Exists 83

Chapter 13: Make Your Budget "A Sophisticated Guide" 93

Chapter 14: Don't Be Afraid to Develop Strategic Partnerships 99

Chapter 15: Marketing Yourself to Market Your Product 105

Section III: Persistence

Chapter 16: Persist and Prevail 117

Chapter 17: "No" Is "Yes" Waiting to Happen 125

Chapter 18: Learn from Failure; Graduate to Success 133

Chapter 19: Be Upbeat or Be Beat Down 139

SECTION IV: PEOPLE

Chapter 20: Have a Caring Attitude Toward All Living Things 147
Chapter 21: Make People Feel Special 151
Chapter 22: Help Others Achieve Their Goals 157
Chapter 23: Managing Perception for Maximum Impact 163
Chapter 24: Create Positive Press 169
Chapter 25: The Power of Trust in Transactions 175
Chapter 26: Don't Burn Bridges (Just Cross Them Carefully the Second Time Around) 181

SECTION V: PHILANTHROPY

Chapter 27: Entrepreneurial Social Responsibility 191
Chapter 28: The Importance of Entrepreneurial Philanthropy 195

SECTION VI: NEW INSIGHTS

Chapter 29: Labor of Love 201
Chapter 30: Friends Who Let You Bend and Break the Rules 215
Chapter 31: Choosing Compatible and Complementary Partners 233

Some Final Thoughts 239
Acknowledgments: No One Creates in a Vacuum 241

APPENDICES

Appendix A: Schussler Creative Inc. Mission Statement 257
Appendix B: The Entrepreneur's Credo 259
Appendix C: The Artist's Credo by Douglas Bloch 261
Appendix D: "Garage" by Erik Calonius, *Fortune* 263

Selected Bibliography 265
About the Author 269
Index 273

PREFACE

For the past 30 years, I've given so many lectures, talks, and workshops about my theory of good business that I can't even count them. My lessons focus on the five Ps of successful entrepreneurship that were discovered through my own experiences: personality, product, persistence, people, and philanthropy. In my life, I've had so much good come out of employing these core strategies. I've launched my dream business, Rainforest Cafe, and watched it grow from an idea everyone thought was crazy into a hugely successful international company. Not only have I made it as a businessman by sticking to what I believe in but also I've been able to share my happiness with millions of kids of all ages who visit my indoor rain forests each year in search of an adventurous dining experience.

At those talks I give on business success strategies, I've been getting the same question over and over: "Steve, where can I buy your book?" I'm a businessman by trade and never thought of myself as an author, so this was something I'd laugh off. I'd leave my business card, figuring the best way to sell my business strategy was with myself—after all, look at the first P, personality—and go on to my next engagement.

But, finally, it hit me like an anvil! Steve, I thought, you're not even listening to yourself in these talks! What's the second P? Product! One of my central strategies for turning Rainforest Cafe into the enormous success it has become is to always anticipate customer needs and interests—it's essential to constantly be on the lookout for products or services people will buy (I talk more about this strategy in chapter 9). Now here were my actual customers of life—my students, the people attending my lectures, and the inspired and aspiring entrepreneurs-to-be—actually *telling* me the product they wanted me to sell them!

Well, this just goes to show you that every day in the business world is a new opportunity to grow and learn. So here I am, writing the second edition of my book—not only purely for the reasons of the business strategies I put forth in it but also in hopes that you, the reader, will be inspired by my story. The truth is I've had an amazing time doing what I love and chasing after my own dreams. In the spirit of the third P, persistence, I never gave up, no matter how unreachable everyone told me those dreams were, and I learned in the end that if you want it badly enough and fight hard enough for it, nothing is out of reach. The idea that I might inspire other people to chase after their own dreams is as exciting as watching my own come true.

Most of the things that I create are highly theatrical and energetic—most projects involve partnering with people who are high-energy entrepreneurs and business professionals. In writing this book, I have tried to capture the energy bounced around during my daily interactions, the thought processes that my team and I create and live by, and my belief in always taking the high road.

My professional life has been a roller-coaster ride, but it's been a fun one. I have reinvented myself many times, which is evidenced by the fact that I held more than a dozen jobs before my sixteenth birthday. I can't stop taking on new projects, thinking of new innovations, and trying out new things that people have avoided trying because they look too difficult or too wild: sometimes they're right and my project comes to nothing, but sometimes they're wrong and I strike upon something truly exciting. I've found that the more I create, the happier I am. The happier I am, the more I create. The two go hand in hand.

Since this book is the story of a guy who's spent that whole roller-coaster ride trying to have fun, I believe that reading it will make you laugh. *It's a Jungle in There* was written to share the entrepreneurial stories from my career that I believe you will find motivational and educational and that will serve as examples of real ways to connect with others who share the same out-of-the-box way of thinking. I share insights on how I look at problems and opportunities that have been everyday occurrences. I have been told that I think differently. I have embraced and documented some of those thought processes with the goal of influencing you to *never give up—no matter what*!

Let me give you an idea of some of the key ideas I'm going to explore in *It's a Jungle in There*. First and foremost is *thank you*. One of the most important lessons I've learned is to give credit where credit is due—the fact is people may work for money, but they live for acknowledgment. By remembering to thank the people who have offered you their time and energy, you make lifelong allies. There are many people who have influenced me. You will hear about some of them throughout the book. I have tried to make certain that those who have touched my life in a significant way were included in the acknowledgments. If I have inadvertently left someone out, I apologize.

The second tenet of business life is taking the high road. My team and I have made a big deal in the book—and in life—about always taking the high road and about giving back. Both of these traits make you a better person and certainly a more successful entrepreneur.

A third key idea is tirelessness—you must keep trying. I use this example when I talk about frequency and consistency in pursuing your goals. When searching for a job, product, or solution to a problem, just remember: the more ships that leave the port to fight the war, the more ships that return. So get out there. Don't send one résumé; send 150. Make sure that there are phone calls and follow-up letters. You just need to do a little bit more and a little bit better than everyone else to be extremely successful.

Fourth is attention to detail, one of the single most important aspects in anything you do. I am known as the "lightbulb nut." I believe lighting is jewelry in our everyday life: our office, our restaurants, my home . . . I cannot stand seeing a lightbulb out. Like a meticulous hotelier, I consider it a measure of attention to detail. If the lightbulb was so obvious, then what else is wrong?

I find myself quite often going into a restaurant, retail store, or business and focusing on the easy fixes that no one else would deem important. Sometimes it is subliminal—your guest or customer might not consciously see it, but he or she feels it! As an entrepreneur, you can make sure you stand out from your competition by never letting the lightbulbs go out.

I can be demanding and loud, but I always try to add humor and thank those around me. I am lucky to have such quality family and friends and such a great team.

As a final note, know that your purchase of this book has an even greater benefit than whatever you get out of the read. I am a founding board member and lifetime advisory board member of Smile Network International. The founder, Kim Valentini, is the true hero of this amazing nonprofit organization. Giving back is something that is the obligation of every entrepreneur, and there are many ways to do so. Working with Smile Network International (www.smilenetwork.org) and sharing my stories with young entrepreneurs are two of the ways that I contribute. A portion of the proceeds from the sale of this book will go to support this cause in addition to a variety of other worthwhile charities and programs.

Steven Schussler shares a banana with some new friends. Taken on a break while constructing the first Rainforest Cafe on Disney Property – Downtown Disney; Orlando, Florida.

SECTION I

PERSONALITY

CHAPTER 1

The Role of Risk-Taking in Entrepreneurial Success

Only those who will risk going too far
can possibly find out how far one can go.

—T. S. Eliot

Self-Examination Question:

Many people prefer to play it safe when it comes to business matters. Are you willing to take risks in the pursuit of entrepreneurial success?

Let me tell you a story about risk taking. When I was eighteen years old, I moved to Miami and got work climbing telephone poles and crawling through sewers as a lineman for Southern Bell Telephone Company. It was hard work for little pay and offered limited opportunities for advancement. When I learned I could make more money *and* build a career for myself selling airtime I knew it was time for me to make a move. The problem was trying to secure a full-time position when I already had one: how could I find the time to call prospective employers and set up interviews?

It took me a few days to come up with a plan. I noticed that all my coworkers were "brown baggers," meaning that they brought their own food to the job site and would climb down the telephone poles during lunchtime to eat. That left me with a window of opportunity. When my colleagues climbed down the poles for lunch, I climbed up, tapping into the phone lines to arrange job interviews. More than once I had to think fast when a homeowner would pick up the phone and hear me on the line. When it happened, I'd say, "Just checking your phone connection," hoping the homeowner would accept my story and hang up before a prospective interviewer got wind of what was happening.

I was able to set up a few appointments, and so I'd climb down the telephone pole at five o'clock and go to my interviews with the station managers. For five months, I went from one interview to the next. The story was always the same: prospective employers told me, "You're the next guy we're going to hire" . . . until I told them my age. Nobody wanted to hire someone so young. So I stopped mentioning my age unless I was specifically asked, and then I'd add a few years to the answer. I looked old for my age; I could have easily passed for a twenty-seven-year-old.

My new approach got positive responses but still no firm job offers. Finally, I decided to take things into my own hands. I wasn't going to take "No" or "We're still considering you" for answers any longer. I was going to do something risky that would either get me hired on the spot or, as my roommate at the time warned, get me incarcerated. (In fact, when he heard my plan, he actually offered me fifty dollars for bail money. "You'll need it if you try and pull *that* off," he warned.)

I wanted to do something so wild and crazy that no one who saw it would ever forget it. I figured the risk was worth it. I wanted to make an impression that had such impact a prospective employer would have no choice but to hire me. And I was convinced that if I could just get past the secretaries and into the boss's office, I could make a showing that would put me on the payroll.

Superman Strategies

Once I decided on my grand strategy to get a job, it took me two days to put my plan into action. The first thing I did was visit a container company, where I purchased a wooden barrel large enough to fit in. Then I went to a costume shop and paid for a Superman outfit, complete with blue tights, red shoes, a cape, and a big S to wear on my chest. My last stop was at the apartment of two friends who happened to be Miami-Dade police officers. I offered them a hundred dollars each to deliver me—tucked inside the barrel—to the office of the station manager where I wanted to work. "You have to be in uniform and use the police paddy wagon to make the delivery," I said, hoping they'd agree. They did.

That night I discussed my plan with my next-door neighbor. She was so concerned I'd get hungry while being transported in the barrel that she fixed me a lunch, comprised of a deli-quality salami sandwich, a pickle, and a can of Diet Coke, to take along on the trip.

The next morning, I put my plan into action. My two officer friends, in full uniform, came to my apartment, stuffed me and my lunch into the barrel, and nailed it shut. Then they took a dolly and loaded me into the police van for the trip across town.

It was just five minutes into the journey that I discovered I had made two grievous errors: one, I hadn't drilled air holes into the barrel, and oxygen was becoming an increasingly scarce commodity; two, I had forgotten how hot Miami can be when you're crammed into a small space and the temperature is registering triple digits. Before long, I was gasping for air and sweating like a pig, and, to make matters worse, the salami sandwich was beginning to stink like a refrigerator full of spoiled food after a power outage. I prayed to God that I wouldn't die in a Superman costume crumpled in a crate; it wasn't the legacy I had imagined for myself.

By the time we finally reached our destination, I was surviving on pure adrenaline and a dogged determination to complete my mission. The cops loaded me on a dolly, wheeled me into Station Manager Don Hamlin's outer office at WGBS Radio, and gave the secretary our prearranged story that they had a shipment of expensive furniture from Mexico for her boss.

I had assumed Hamlin would be there. That was my near-fatal error. As it turned out, he was attending a board meeting with the company's top executives in a hotel across the street.

I couldn't hear anything while sealed inside the barrel, but, fortunately, my friends persisted. They told the secretary they couldn't leave the furniture without the boss's signature. They urged her to call him on the phone, which she finally agreed to do. I was told later the conversation went like this:

"Mr. Hamlin, we have two policemen here with some expensive furniture you ordered from Mexico. They can't leave until you sign for it in person."

"Are you crazy? I didn't order any furniture from Mexico. And I've got twenty board members here!"

"Well, what should I do?"

"I'm coming right over, and there better be an explanation for all this."

At this point, I'd probably lost ten pounds from sweating, I smelled like a dead animal, and a crowd was gathering. To make matters worse, the Diet Coke I was holding had exploded from the heat, hurtling foam, soda, and salami fragments over my hair, face, and costume.

A few agonizing minutes later, Don Hamlin, followed by his entire board of directors, marched into the office. "What the hell is this all about?" he shouted as my friends pried the nails from the barrel and prepared to lift off the top.

At this point, I was thinking, "This is either going to be the best or the worst day of my life." I was also thinking if I didn't get a breath of air in the next thirty seconds, it would be the *last* day of my life.

As the lid slid away from the barrel, I came flying out like a jack-in-the-box, gasping for air and wiping Coke and salami from my eyes. The stench from the barrel filled the room.

I smiled at everyone and said, "Hello, everybody, my name is Steve Schussler. I'm your new super salesman." Then I went around and shook each person's hand. The board members were in various stages of shock. Finally, the oldest guy—he must have been eighty years old—pointed at me with his cane and said, "Son, you are the sickest person we've ever met. You're hired."

Steven Schussler before his "Super Salesman" pitch to Mr. Don Hamlin at WGBS radio of Miami Beach.

Steven Schussler with associates from WKAT All Talk Radio in Miami Beach.

I know what some of you are thinking: "That Superman gambit was a *really* risky maneuver." And you're right. Anytime you play Superman-in-a-barrel, it involves risk. Fortunately, some of this risk can be reduced by better understanding how those affected by your actions will most likely react to them. In my case, I had the advantage of being interviewed twice by Don Hamlin—the radio station manager who eventually hired me—and had been able to determine that he had a sense of humor. That knowledge helped me formulate my plan. It was because I felt Don would appreciate an off-the-wall approach that I tried the Superman stunt in the first place.

If you want to be a successful entrepreneur, you have to be a risk taker. Passion, ambition, and talent are all traits that help a businessperson make it to the top, as you need all three to work your way up the corporate totem pole. But you need guts to be in business for yourself.

A successful businessperson operating in a corporate environment is like an acrobat doing all kinds of elaborate tricks on a high wire. Sure, it's impressive, but he or she has a safety harness on. Where's the danger in that? Entrepreneurship is like performing a steady walk across two forty-foot-high platforms. It doesn't have to involve fancy footwork; it can be just moving gingerly along the taut wire strung forty feet above the arena floor. What makes the performance impressive is that lack of a safety net.

The successful businessperson can't worry about falling. You can't worry about falling. There's no room for the faint of heart, for the risk-averse player, in the entrepreneurial game. When it comes to your career, there's a good chance you'll experience some bumps and bruises along the way, even some ego-crushing and wallet-flattening descents from high places. But there is great reward, and satisfaction, awaiting the entrepreneur who can handle risk, walk the wire between failure and success, and come out a winner on the other side.

Risky Business

I found out firsthand the risks inherent in starting your own business. It happened in Chicago when I was in my twenties. I had a good job selling television advertising. But there was a problem. One day, I calculated that I was making $4 to $5 million for the company but getting only 0.0085 percent back in commissions for my efforts. It didn't seem fair. I was working sixteen hours a day creating a lot of wealth for someone else. I realized that I might do better if I was on my own.

At the same time I was questioning my pay (or lack of it), I happened to visit an antique shop where I spotted a broken-down vintage Wurlitzer jukebox. It was one of the old, fancy art deco kinds, with lots of neon and bubbles flowing through translucent cylinders that bordered the front of the machine. The owner offered to sell it to me for five hundred dollars. I told him it was wrecked, but that didn't faze him. "I'll tell you where you can get all the parts you need to fix it up," he told me. "Once you do that, it'll be worth five thousand dollars." Despite my doubts, I took him up on the offer.

It took me less than twenty-four hours to experience a severe case of buyer's remorse. The jukebox was more damaged than I'd originally thought, so I went back to the store to try to get a refund. The guy refused. I had no choice but to buy the parts and get the thing working.

It turned out I actually enjoyed doing the work to restore it. Then I turned around and sold the jukebox for forty-five hundred dollars! Considering that it cost only one thousand for the parts, plus the original five hundred I paid, I was showing a healthy profit—a far better return on my investment than I was receiving with my real job.

I became passionate about jukeboxes and other antiques, particularly old carousel horses and slot machines. I learned everything I could about their cost, worth, and history as collectables. I spent time repairing and restoring them, getting them into the kind of shape that would attract buyers and provide me with a nice profit margin. I became so convinced I had found a niche market that I figured I could turn my newfound hobby into a business.

I decided to rent a store where I could sell the nostalgia items I had restored and call it JukeBox Saturday Night. I found some commercial space and started moving things in. I assumed I'd be able to get everything up and running in a weekend, but it took longer than expected. As a result, I took off Monday as a sick day from work to finish things up.

It's hard to explain the excitement I felt when I heard my new business phone ring for the first time that Monday afternoon. Here I was, about to do business in my very own place. I was amazed: my listing in the yellow pages had yet to be published, the store wasn't listed in any directories, I hadn't done any advertising . . . and yet word must have gotten out that JukeBox was opening. What a start!

"JukeBox Saturday Night," I answered proudly. "Can I help you?"

Turns out I couldn't. Worse, it turned out that the caller was my TV sales manager, who had found out about my business venture and unceremoniously fired me on the spot. Now that I was out of a job, I was truly an entrepreneur. I had taken a risk, and now I felt like the ground had just caved in. I had no income, and I'd just taken out a hundred-thousand-dollar loan against my condo.

Things went downhill from there. People loved my store, and they'd stop in and admire the stuff like they were in a museum, but nobody bought anything. I had to file for bankruptcy. In lieu of foreclosure, I surrendered my condo, and my company truck was repossessed. I was so poor I had to wear the same clothes for days in a row. I ended up living in a small nine-by-twelve-foot office above the dance floor of a place called the Rodeo Nightclub. I was jammed in with my inventory of antiques and my sheepdog. Forced to listen to honky-tonk music until four o'clock in the morning, my poor dog was driven crazy by the crammed quarters and loud music. He, in a frenzy, lashed out and bit me, sending me to the hospital where I got so bored being confined to my bed that I made it my goal to come up with a hundred new ways to make my JukeBox Saturday Night name and idea a success.

One of those ideas panned out. I ended up joining with the owner of the Rodeo Nightclub, Jimmy Rittenberg, to develop a 1950s retro dance club, decorating it with the jukeboxes and other antiques from my defunct store. At least I got one thing out of my failed store: we took its name and called our new club and restaurant JukeBox Saturday Night.

The venture turned out to be a huge success. We opened four establishments in Chicago, Illinois and expanded to Des Moines, Iowa; San Francisco, California; Springfield, Massachusetts; and

Minneapolis , Minnesota. I ended up moving to Minneapolis to manage the JukeBox there. With the profits we were making, it felt like we were literally minting money. I felt great. My initial risk, trying to be an entrepreneur while holding down a regular job, was costly. I was fired, suffered economic hardship, and was even mauled by my own dog. But, in the long run, the risk was well worth it because it forced me to find a new way to make a living and gave me the opportunity to find my true calling in life. I became a creator of attractions, themed restaurants, and retail stores—a passion that occupies my mind and captures my heart to this day.

Risk taking is, at least to me, part of what being an entrepreneur is all about. There are probably some successful risk-aversive businesspeople out there who would take issue with me, but, ultimately, I truly believe that if it's not worth the risk, it's probably not worth the reward.

Jimmy Rittenberg, affectionately nicknamed the "Prince of Fun," was responsible for helping Steven turn his retail store, Jukebox Saturday Night, into a night club chain with eight locations in Chicago, Illinois; Des Moines, Iowa; San Francisco, California; and Minneapolis, Minnesota.

Steven Schussler sits on a '57 Chevy underneath the entrance of the Jukebox Saturday Night in Minneapolis, Minnesota.

The Jukebox Saturday Night club in Minneapolis, Minnesota, was featured on the front cover of Architecture Minnesota after receiving the magazine's 1984 Honor Award.

CHAPTER 2

The Importance of Passion

"Passion makes perfect."

—Eugene Biro

Self-Examination Question:

If you were independently wealthy and never had to work a day in your life, would you still choose to spend your time attempting to become a successful entrepreneur?

Back in the 1990s, a friend sent me a statement someone wrote on the topic of passion. I use it as an introduction to all my speeches on entrepreneurship because it captures the essence of how important passion is for success in business and in life. It says, "Passion Is the Engine of Success."

Passion is called by many names: drive, desire, hunger, and motivation. Passion is the power that is released to take action when someone feels intense about someone or something. As a leadership quality, one's own passion is what galvanizes others into action.

Of this I am absolutely certain: the business of hospitality is centered on one's passion for pleasing people. Passion is the fuel for tenacity, perseverance, and attention to detail. It energizes the body and mind to overcome fatigue, fear, and failure. It is the fuel that allows individuals to cope with challenging conditions. One common weakness I find in management (and educators) is overlooking the power of this awesome emotion in their search for prospective leaders and teachers. One can argue that passion alone is not enough, but to lack passion is to lack a vital ingredient for obtaining compliance and team building and, thus, success.

Don't ever be dissuaded from being passionate about your work. Those of you who measure work not in terms of hours but in achievement and pleasure, the ones working sixty to eighty hours a week because you love it, you are marching to the beat of a different drummer in today's society. You really have what it takes to make a difference in the world. Most of all, you have what it takes to make a difference in the lives of the people you touch. You will often find this place in which you exist lonely. Don't be deterred by the frequent urges of your peers to "Get a life" or "Take it easy or you're going to kill yourself." Life's great fulfillment exists in the pursuit of achieving . . . and that endless pursuit is fueled by passion.

The Power of Passion

It is no accident that all the business books I've ever read include passion as one of the critical factors shaping individual success in the workplace. Passion is a basic requisite for aspiring entrepreneurs: it will allow them to overcome the hardships, failures, challenges, doubts, and uncertainties that come with the territory. Passion is the force that drives people to do their best, to make a difference.

I'm not talking about your run-of-the-mill, everyday kind of desires that all people have; those yearnings don't rise to the level of the driving force that shapes the way people live their lives. I'm talking about PASSION. I'm talking about the "Give me liberty or give me death" kind of passion, the "I've got a dream" kind of passion, the "I love you, Juliet" kind of passion. I'm talking about the difference between liking something and loving something, about people who don't just do what they like but love what they do, about not going through the motions but going through *with emotions*. I'm talking about people like Albert Schweitzer, Mother Teresa, Mahatma Gandhi—people with a long-term passion for what they are doing. These are the kind of people Ferdinand Foch was referring to when he said, "The most powerful weapon on earth is the human soul on fire."

Are you passionate about your work? Here's one way to find out: Pretend that you just won fifty million dollars in the lottery and find yourself financially secure for the rest of your life. Now that you have financial independence and don't ever have to earn an income to live comfortably, what would you want to do with the rest of your life?

Whatever you choose to do is probably something you are passionate about doing. Confucius once said, "Choose a job you love and you will never have to work a day in your life." That's the way entrepreneurs have to feel about what they are doing: they have to have a love for their labor, a passion for what they are trying to achieve. Passion is the fuel that keeps entrepreneurs moving ahead. It gives them the strength to push forward when others say they will be left behind, to persevere when the flashing light says, "Abandon ship!" Passion is the ingredient that, when mixed with committed human effort, gives the entrepreneur the opportunity to demonstrate that "impossible" is "I'm possible" waiting to be discovered. Without that passion, an entrepreneur is going to end up an *exit*preneur.

One reason I became an entrepreneur was that I realized a lot of people I worked with weren't particularly happy with their jobs and yet they didn't do anything about it. I thought that was hypocritical, and I was determined not to turn out like them. They would complain every day that their sales commissions were being cut or the people they were dealing with or working for weren't ethical. They just felt victimized all the time. I said to myself, "I'm going to take the risk and go out on my own."

Always remember: passion is critical to success. I believe if you love what you're doing, you're going to do it well. And, come to think of it, if you don't enjoy what you're doing, what good is it if you do well, anyway? We spend, on average, forty-five years of our adult lives in the workplace. Life's simply too short to feel bad about your job.

Build It and They Will Come

When you are passionate about a project, anything is possible.

As an example: for years, I wanted to create a themed restaurant based on the tropical rain forest. It started back when I was a teenager. I loved parrots and fish, and I wanted to have a restaurant where they could be displayed for interactive, educational purposes. I also wanted to create an environmental awareness of these beautiful creatures and educate people about what they could do to save the rain forest. The problem was getting investors interested in my idea. Just talking about the project was getting me nowhere. I had to do something far more dramatic and impactful if I ever wanted a shot at financial backing for my idea.

My attention-grabbing idea? I turned my suburban home into a tropical rain forest. I created a jungle in my home smack dab in the middle of my residential neighborhood. Over a period of several years, my standard split-level home was transformed into a jungle dwelling complete with rock outcroppings, waterfalls, rivers, layers of fog, mist that rose from the ground, a thatched hut covered with vines on the roof, tiki torches, a twelve-foot neon "paradise" sign, and a full-size replica of an elephant near the front door.

It wasn't easy to create this life-size prototype. I had to knock out rooms to create a greenhouse, and I purchased 3,700 bright orange extension cords to hook up to the twenty different sound systems, lights, and fog pumps that provided the jungle noise and mist that floated through the house. Then I had to learn to live with forty tropical birds, two 150-pound tortoises, a baboon, an iguana, and a bevy of tropical fish housed in ten three-hundred-gallon tanks. There were also fifty different animatronic creatures in the house—a collection of mechanized alligators, gorillas, and monkeys. At least I didn't have to feed or clean up after them, but changing their batteries was a real chore. I finally devised a way to get them to run on electricity.

In the bedroom, my bed was constructed to look like it was suspended in a tree. It had waterfalls behind it, and mist rose up in different places throughout the room. Live birds and animals moved freely through the area during showings of the house. There were tortoises in the kitchen, parrots in the bathroom, and fish everywhere. The humidity from the pumped-in fog and mist destroyed the wallpaper, but I didn't care. Every room, every closet, every hallway of my house was a *scene*: an attempt to present my idea of what a rain forest restaurant would look like in actual operation. My house became one huge theatrical set, a life-size presentation of my vision for Rainforest Cafe. Overall, it took me three years and almost four hundred thousand dollars to get the house developed to the point where I felt comfortable showing it to potential investors.

Several of my neighbors weren't exactly thrilled to be living near a jungle habitat. They started a watch group. They even bought walkie-talkies to update one another on what was happening. One day, the front entry chimed, and I opened the door to what looked like a full-scale crime scene. There were cop cars and officers all over the place. One guy put me up against the door and said he was with the Drug Enforcement Administration and they were going to search the premises for drugs. Because of my huge residential electric bill, they assumed I was growing marijuana in the house. They were astonished when they discovered the tropical rain forest.

Let me tell you: it's not easy to live in a house filled with jungle creatures and surrounded by angry neighbors, all on the off chance that it might secure funding for an entrepreneurial dream. What got

Steven's love of birds and primates began as a teenager during his trips to Acapulco, Mexico.

me through was passion, pure and simple. I knew no venture capitalists were going to invest their money in my far-out concept without seeing and experiencing it themselves. So I transformed my house into my vision of a rain forest restaurant in order to make them believe in my dream.

It's a Jungle in There

My plan eventually succeeded. A fellow Minnesotan, gaming executive and venture capitalist Lyle Berman, bought into the concept and raised the funds necessary to get Rainforest Cafe up and running.

I remember every detail of the first time Lyle visited my home. It was early morning, and he stopped by on his way to work. I came out to greet him wearing jeans and a khaki shirt, like a safari guide, with a parrot on my shoulder. I led him inside, where he was greeted by forty tropical birds in cages, a live tortoise, and a baby baboon named Charlie wearing a dress. Jungle foliage, including all kinds of plants and vines, hung from every surface. There was a thirty-five-foot waterfall, too, which emptied into a river that snaked through the house and out into the yard. It was filled with pink antifreeze so it wouldn't stop flowing in the winter. To top it off, I created a mock-up of a retail store with various kinds of rain forest merchandise. It looked like a Florida souvenir shop on steroids.

Potential Rainforest Cafe investors were driven to the entrance of Steven's home in fun cars lit with tiki torches. Caribbean music played in the background to complete the scene. The cars were converted transportation carts from an old playland amusement park.

The entrance of the Rainforest Cafe prototype in Steven's home, complete with a neon "Paradise" sign, mists, elephant statues, live exotic birds, and erupting waterfall

At night, the Rainforest Cafe comes alive with theatrical lighting.

The current thunder and lightning shows at the Rainforest Cafe restaurants were first built in Steven's bedroom, which featured simulated tropical rainfalls and thunderstorms; frogs, birds, and animated monkeys; and a lush canopy of leaves, vines, and lights over the bed.

After giving Lyle a tour of the house, I asked him what he thought of it. He told me I needed a psychiatric examination and there was no way he'd invest in my idea. He then asked whether he could bring his kids by to see the house, to which I of course agreed. On his next visit, after giving his kids the grand tour, I again asked Lyle what he thought of my idea.

"Well, your dedication and passion are off the chart," he admitted, "but I'm not buying into this." Then he asked whether he could bring his parents over.

By the time Lyle's parents completed the tour, Lyle and I had developed a little ritual. Once the visit was over, I'd ask him what he thought. Then I'd anxiously await his answer. This time I reminded Lyle how committed I was to the project, and his response was "I think you should *be* committed!"

As time passed, Lyle found additional reasons to visit my house. I guess my tenacity and passion for the Rainforest Cafe idea grew on him. He kept visiting my house, bringing over other investors for their reactions. He even brought a bus full of his employees for a tour. Finally, after about two years, Lyle decided to back my idea, and the rest is history: the Rainforest Cafe chain went public with only one unit open and became one of the most successful themed restaurant concepts ever created. It continues that way today under Landry's Restaurants and Tilman Fertitta's leadership.

These days, of course, I create my restaurant concepts in office buildings and warehouses far from residential neighborhoods, but back then there were no warehouses. I sunk every dollar I had into making my house a themed rain forest restaurant because I was passionate about the concept and wanted to see it become a reality.

Lyle Berman, the angel investor who provided the funding to make Steven's dream of Rainforest Cafe a reality, at the Renaissance Festival in Shakopee, Minnesota. Steven's red scarlet macaw and blue hyacinth birds, Jules and Little Boy, rest on his shoulders.

Steven with his favorite bird, Little Boy, on the roof of his home and Rainforest Cafe prototype.

Passion Trumps Problems

There were times when I truly wondered whether my rain forest dream would ever become a reality. After Lyle visited the house more than twenty times in two years without committing himself, you can be damn sure I was frustrated. That's when I decided to make up a sign saying, "Lyle Berman made me do this!" and told him if he didn't buy into my restaurant concept, I was going to hang the sign around my neck and jump off the Hennepin Avenue Bridge. (No, I don't think I would have jumped . . . but I would have invited Lyle over for another visit.) That's where passion kicked in. When you're passionate about what you're doing, you'll do whatever needs to be done to reach your objective, to attain your goal. Failure isn't an option; the word "no" isn't in your vocabulary.

Being passionate doesn't totally shield you from moments of doubt, unfortunately. There were nights I'd go to bed and have trouble sleeping. I remember looking in the mirror and wondering whether I really was crazy. I told myself I was neurotic. It was an emotional time for me. I didn't know how long I could keep things going; I just knew Rainforest Cafe was a great idea, and I couldn't let it go. I wanted to share my passion for the tropical rain forest with everyone.

Of course, the DEA raid hadn't helped matters, but it wasn't my biggest headache. (In fact, when the agents found out what was really in the house, several of them brought their kids over to visit, and some even purchased stock in the company.) No, the worst moment for me involved a disagreement with the gas company. It was over bills. I hadn't been paying them, and, even more troublesome, I reconnected the gas meter a few times after the company had turned it off for nonpayment.

Things came to a head one Friday night when a convoy of trucks showed up in the cul-de-sac where my house was located. It was the gas company. I guess management was tired of me finding ways to turn the gas back on. The workers dug a twenty-five-foot-deep hole in the road and shut off the main gas valve to my house. Then they covered up the hole and prepared the road to be repaved.

I was desperate! It was the beginning of winter, and the gas supplied heat to the house. Without it, my animals would die. Luckily, it wasn't too cold yet, and we were able to get by with electric heaters. I called the gas company and begged its representatives to turn the gas back on. It took me three days to raise the money to get the workers to come back. I ended up having to pay the bill plus the cost of digging and repaving the road. The neighbors were none too happy, either. Believe me, that was one time when even *my* passion wavered a bit. But, in the final analysis, I picked myself up and moved on, reminding myself of the words penned by Arthur Buddhold: "Follow your passion, and success will follow you." That's how Rainforest Cafe was born.

And that's why I make no apologies for living passionately, and neither should you.

The first Rainforest Cafe on Disney property featured live tropical birds at its entrance.

Steven at the grand opening of the first Rainforest Cafe on October 3, 1994, at the Mall of America in Bloomington, Minnesota.

The first Rainforest Cafe on Disney property, at Downtown Disney in Orlando, Florida, features a dramatic erupting volcano.

Boathouse guests can admire the Rainforest Cafe volcano and its striking reflection on Lake Buena Vista.

CHAPTER 3

Ambition: Taking Your Passions Public

Ambition is the germ from which all growth of nobleness proceeds.

—Thomas Dunn

Self-Examination Question:

Do you desire and/or seek public recognition for what you have created?

There are individuals who think ambition is a bad thing. Perhaps that's why, for some people, the term has a negative connotation, conjuring up images of backstabbing corporate climbers. I'm not one of these individuals. I believe that ambition, like passion, drives people to realize their full potential: to become all they are capable of in both their personal and business lives.

I didn't come from a rich home. In fact, we had to scrimp and save just to make ends meet. Yet I was able to realize my dream of becoming a successful entrepreneur because I was ambitious. Driven to succeed, when I was young, I would get up earlier than all my friends and go to work. By the time they awoke, around eleven o'clock in the morning, I had already been working for four hours and had twenty dollars stashed in my pocket. Today, I continue to get up and work hours before my other team members show up at the office. It's those hours before nine o'clock in the morning that have made the crucial difference in my success.

Of course, being born wealthy hardly hurts a person's chances of succeeding in today's competitive world, but it is neither necessary nor sufficient to guarantee success. If you are short on cash but long on ambition, limited in funds but unlimited in your commitment to get ahead and make a name for yourself, you can achieve greatness. Desire beats dollars every day of the week. I'd rather bet on a person with ambition than on someone with money who thinks the world owes him or her a living. I'll take commitment over cash every time when it comes to predicting entrepreneurial success. For those with ambition, the good news is the "American Dream" is alive and well: you needn't be born with a silver spoon in your mouth to achieve a generous portion of success in your life.

In my opinion, being hungry, feeling economically pinched, can actually stimulate the creative juices and fire up a person to achieve more than someone who is financially comfortable and just doesn't have the same level of need to produce something of significance. Maybe that's why the concept of the "starving artist" resonates with me. In fact, maybe that's what the term is all about: being without, being willing to forego normal creature comforts in search of perfection in one's work.

Passion + Ambition Yields Success (It P.A.Y.S.)!

In my seminars and discussions with other businesspeople, I'm often surprised that people either don't see the importance of ambition for entrepreneurial success or treat "passion" and "ambition" as the same thing. In fact, passion and ambition have a symbiotic relationship when it comes to entrepreneurs. Think of passion and ambition as the peanut butter and jelly of entrepreneurial success: they work together to create a better outcome. Passion provides the fuel that drives a person to create a service or product, and ambition supplies the desire to get that service or product out to the public. Without ambition, a passionate person might create great things but not have the urge to share them.

I knew a writer who was that way. He loved to write and had a passion for his craft. He would sit day after day at his computer creating works of fiction, but he'd never try to get them published. When I asked him about his reluctance to share his books with others, he said the satisfaction of writing was reward enough for him. But was that it? Who knows? Perhaps he was afraid of rejection or public reaction to his work. Whatever the reason, here was a man with a passion who lacked the ambition to bring his creations into a bigger world. He was like the proverbial tree that fell in the forest with no one there to hear it.

Most people aren't like my friend the writer. If they produce something they believe has value, they'll try to market it. What varies mightily is the degree of effort they will expend to get the most from their discovery or product. Ambitious people will push what they have to the limit, while people of less ambition—though they might have something of equal value—will have a lesser marketplace impact.

Passion by itself isn't enough. Producing the greatest invention or work of art on Earth isn't enough. To me, it doesn't become significant until the person of passion who created it has enough ambition to share it with others. That is the critical link between passion and ambition and why both must be present in people who want to reach their full potential as entrepreneurs.

Many years ago I came across something called "The Artist's Credo" by Douglas Bloch, who wrote *Listening to Your Inner Voice.* It represents how I feel about art and the artistic product. One portion of that credo is germane to the relationship between passion and ambition (see p. 261 for the credo in full):

> *After the creation is born, it needs to be shared with others. No one creates in a vacuum. It is only when the vision is successfully communicated to its intended audience that it truly comes alive.*

Sadly, in most cases, passion without ambition is passion wasted. Successful entrepreneurship requires both the creation of a valued product or service and its public introduction into the marketplace. Entrepreneurs with a lack of ambition to share the fruits of their passion will never be as successful as entrepreneurs with the passion and ambition to bring their creations to the attention of the consuming public.

Ambition helps passion succeed. As J. C. Penney once said, "Give me a stock clerk with a goal and I'll give you a man who will make history. Give me a man with no goals and I'll give you a stock clerk."

CHAPTER 4

I Dream . . . Therefore I Can

Happy are those who dream dreams and are ready to pay the price to make them come true.

—Leon Joseph Cardinal Suenens

Self-Examination Question:

Do you take joy in dreaming up new ideas, products, or services that have profit potential in the marketplace?

Entrepreneurs possess the ability to see things that others have not yet envisioned. Passion serves as the springboard for making these dreams tangible. When you allow yourself to feel truly passionate about something, it spawns ideas, and those lead to other ideas, and then, if you're me, you have a room full of dinosaurs in your office and a booming business behind them.

Of course, not all dreams are created equal. When I'm speaking of "dreams" in the context of entrepreneurial success, I'm not referring to the kind of dreams people have while sleeping (although some ideas have come during such moments) or to daydreams, where individuals are simply entertaining themselves with fantasies that have no economic implications. In the vast majority of cases, the dreams that bring business success are those experienced by entrepreneurs as they allow their imaginations free rein in experiencing what goes on around them in their everyday lives. That leads them to think about what services or products they might create to bring value and improve lives in a manner that would bring them financial gain.

An interesting example of how the dream process works to spur entrepreneurial endeavors and success is provided in the movie *Bugsy*, where the main character (played by Warren Beatty) is driving across the Mojave Desert and suddenly stops his car to get out. He peers into the desert wasteland, considers the desolation all around him, and envisions a gambling casino that eventually turns Las Vegas into the gaming capital of the world.

I experienced a parallel example of this creative process while crossing the South Dakota Badlands on my motorcycle. I, too, stopped along the side of the deserted road, and, as I stared into the desolate terrain, I saw a place where dinosaurs once roamed. I pictured a restaurant based on the giant beasts. That image eventually morphed into the highly successful T-REX in Disney World.

My office is in Minneapolis, which is not a big city like New York City or Chicago. But it hasn't affected my inspiration and enthusiasm.

You could be a kid on a farm in Iowa milking cows, and, if you're willing to dream, you can dream as large as anyone, anywhere.

In fact, it can work to your advantage. Here, in the land of ten thousand lakes, I'm continually inspired by magnificent wooden boats on these beautiful bodies of water. You don't get to see these boats on the ocean because the salt eats away at the wood. In the summer, these dream boats are everywhere, inspiring me with the nostalgia, craftsmanship, and history they embody.

Dreaming also means nurturing the ability to see what others cannot and training your mind to see and do what other people do not notice.

Entrepreneurs must be willing to work for their dreams. They must be constantly on the lookout for that new idea, new service, new product, or new angle. They must realize that conceiving an idea not only is the necessary first step to entrepreneurial success—but also is often the most important part of the journey. Don't be afraid to give your mind free rein. As Anthony Robbins wisely observes, "To achieve the impossible, it is precisely the unthinkable that must be thought." *If you knew you could not fail, what would you attempt to do?*

Don't be afraid to dream and dream big. It is the unusual person who knows the value of planning big, shooting high, and keeping his or her eyes wide open for opportunities.

Successful entrepreneurs are disposed to be optimists; they have the adventurous and fearless attitude that allows them to dream and not get bogged down by naysayers and doubters who would challenge their inspirations. Entrepreneurs are, in many ways, futurists. That is, they love to live in the future, dream about the future, talk about the future—and they are always urging people around them to do the same.

One might wonder whether there is ever a time that an aspiring entrepreneur should think "small" when looking for a successful venture. I believe the personal character and creative process of individual entrepreneurs play a role in determining whether they want to aim for a little piece of the Earth or shoot for the stars. It's in my nature to "think big." Why would you want sales of $850,000 a year owning a small pizzeria when you could use the same amount of hard work and passion to earn much more? It takes just as much time and energy to run a business that grosses $850,000 in sales as one that grosses thirty million dollars. Your passion, ambition, and energy do not change because of the gross income you are expecting.

Dreaming big also gives a person a better chance at succeeding big. When Michael Phelps won a record-shattering eight gold medals in the Beijing Olympics, he said, "I saw quotes that [Mark] Spitz's seven medals record would be impossible to duplicate, that it would never happen. But if you dream as big as you can dream, anything is possible."

As a "dream-driven" entrepreneur working in a capitalist system where dreams can still come true, one should never underestimate the importance of dreams. Use the power of your mind to incubate, nourish, and bring your dreams to fruition. Remember that the Lord gave us two ends: one to sit on and one to think with. Success depends on which one you use—heads you win, tails you lose!

One of the most inspiring articles I ever read was published in *Fortune* magazine back in 1996. It describes how some of America's greatest entrepreneurs—people like Henry Ford, Walt Disney, C. E. Woolman (Delta Airlines), and Steve Jobs—built their dreams into dynasties by developing their ideas in the obscurity of their garages. The article can be found in the appendix at the end of this book.

Always remember that some of the most memorable and successful entrepreneurial undertakings started with a dream. Keep dreams foremost in your entrepreneurial arsenal and you will always have creative firepower at your disposal. I think this poem by Langston Hughes says it all:

Hold fast to dreams
For if dreams die
Life is a broken-winged bird
That cannot fly.
Hold fast to dreams
For when dreams go
Life is a barren field
Frozen with snow.

CHAPTER 5

The Multitasker

A person who learns to juggle six balls will be more skilled than the person who never tries to juggle more than three.

—Marilyn Vos Savant

Self-Examination Question:

Can you comfortably and successfully perform two or more tasks at the same time?

A long time ago, a client walked into my office for the first time and saw me sitting at my desk. "You looked like the mission control guy they cut to on CNN when the Space Shuttle crew says something important, like 'Houston, I think we have a problem,'" he told me later. "You were speaking into a cell phone in one hand while checking your BlackBerry in the other. I looked at your desk and saw three different computer screens, each run by a separate computer. There were also three separate landline phones within reach." (In fact, the client had failed to notice a laptop computer lying on the floor, a television, two fax machines, and—to complete the communication cornucopia—a designated "red phone" with a direct international line to my home in Acapulco, Mexico.)

All that communication equipment is on my desk for a purpose. I use it! It's not unusual for me to carry on two, three, or even four conversations at the same time while tracking the computer screens on my desk. It's called "multitasking," and it's a skill I believe all entrepreneurs will need to have if they want to stay competitive in the new realities of computer- and smartphone-driven business in the twenty-first century.

When it comes to multitasking, I guess I'm one of the lucky ones. I seem to have the personality for it. Ever since I was a kid, people would notice my short attention span and restless need to keep "several balls in the air." I was always doing multiple things at once. As I grew older, psychologists began giving my behavior a name: attention deficit disorder (ADD). They were usually referring to my habit of doing several things at once, often in a hyper (or, as I like to think of it, highly energetic) fashion. This "hyper-tasking" is quite satisfying, yet some of my friends and business associates think I should avoid doing it. One of my partners once warned me, "If you take your eyes off the ball and people think the creator of Rainforest Cafe is developing other concepts, they're going to think you're a flake. Our stock prices are going to go down, so let's just make this one work. They will think you lost your passion or direction."

My partner could not envision a person driven passionately about more than one project at a time. The fact is that I *was* keeping my eye on the ball; it's just that, like a juggler, I happened to have several balls in the air at the time. In fact, I firmly believe that one of the most important talents (or skills) an entrepreneur can have is the ability to multitask. Entrepreneurs often have three or four or five things going on simultaneously. It's a disservice to tell them that they should be focused, because they *are* focused—it's just that they are also thinking on multiple levels. They can track six balls at once. It's a gift, and they should embrace it.

Thinking on multiple levels works for me because it stimulates my creative juices. If I want to think about custom motorcycles one day and French saxophone players the next, let me do that. If I'm at the Tuscan Gem, Mineral and Fossil Showcase in Arizona researching for T-REX, why can't I find something that would work in my Asian restaurant concept as well? If I see butterflies at the state fair and the sight gives me an idea for a chandelier, why can't I pursue that? That's my prerogative. When researching, it is a talent and gift to let your mind be challenged and envision two thoughts at once. It is okay to get off track and take advantage of a new thought.

But here is the true value of multitasking: it allows you to have several concepts or ideas going at once. That means that, when investors come knocking, you don't have just one shot to get their business; you have several opportunities. It's like a car dealership: there's more than one model to choose from, which gives customers more choices—and thus a greater chance they'll find something that suits them.

On several occasions, my ability to multitask is what has been directly responsible for landing major deals. For instance, when Disney became interested in our T-REX restaurant, they also liked our Asian concept, Yak & Yeti. They told me they would do T-REX only if they could have the Asian restaurant, too. Well, I certainly didn't complain about that requirement. If I hadn't been working on five concepts at once, that deal never would have happened. Other times, I've walked investors through my warehouses and they've passed by three concepts with no interest—only to buy into the fourth.

Yak & Yeti, a Pan-Asian restaurant created by Steven Schussler, owned by Landry's Restaurant Inc. and Steven Schussler, and operated by Landry's Restaurant Inc. at Disney's Animal Kingdom in Orlando, Florida.

The point is that my multitasking ability allows me to give investors a greater opportunity to invest in our projects by providing more choices to our current and potential business partners.

Of course, there are challenges associated with multitasking. One of the most difficult multitasking skills is not losing attention to detail. Many multitaskers try to do so much that they lose focus on the specifics. What makes a successful multitasker is being able to handle many things at the same time while still being able to focus on exquisite, explicit detail. That can be anything from the flowers that go on a table for a presentation to the smell that's in the air to the music that's playing in the background.

Another is the ability to prioritize on the fly and, if need be, to change those priorities as you go. What's first? What's second? Why are they in that order? Do you have the ability to switch and make what was once fourth on your list first because someone just telephoned you and its importance suddenly jumped? Multitasking doesn't mean juggling a number of issues and ideas; it's knowing which of those issues and ideas matter the most—and recognizing when those priorities shift.

Many people criticize multitaskers—saying if you can't pay attention to one specific thing, you can't maintain the ability to focus on many details at once. If you're good at multitasking, nothing could be further from the truth. You know exactly what you're doing and why—that just happens to involve more than one thing at a time.

And, bear in mind that, in some cases, people are critical of multitaskers because they can't do it themselves. If you're good at multitasking, leverage it to your advantage. Don't ever apologize for it.

Whether you're just starting your entrepreneurial career or you're a seasoned veteran, when people tell you to focus on one thing at a time and stop multitasking, don't listen! You have a special talent, and you should be grateful that you do. The future belongs to us multitaskers, so keep on juggling with a smile on your face.

CHAPTER 6

Layer, Then Layer Some More

When you're directing something, you absolutely have to be involved in all layers of the process.

—Cate Blanchett

Self-Examination Question:

When you create something, do you consistently improve on what you've done?

An entrepreneur without something to sell is like a consumer with no money to buy. It's a losing proposition. Without the ability to create a marketable service or product, any would-be entrepreneur is doomed to fail. Even the most well-intentioned, passionate, ambitious individual can't make the sale if he or she has nothing to offer.

This is where dreaming comes in. Whether you are an aspiring or established entrepreneur, you should always be dreaming of new ways to make your mark on the world. Don't be afraid to dream big.

And be sure to continually add layers to what you create.

Here's what I mean by layering. When I was in high school, I worked for a florist. There I learned how to design floral arrangements. It's about layering, spirals, and building things up, down, and sideways.

But layers aren't used for the sake of simply adding something. When you layer something, you're taking what you already have and making it better.

My life, including everything I design and create, revolves around layering. When I first created the Rainforest Cafe prototype in my home, I layered the canopy with honeysuckle, grapevines, ropes, swinging monkeys, other animals, and, finally, Spanish moss.

Lighting is a type of architectural jewelry and an essential feature of layering. In one room, we might use five or six different kinds of lighting. We use architectural lighting, theatrical lighting, uplighting, downlighting, security lighting, and cleaning lighting. The many layers of lighting are crucial to making a fully functioning creative idea come to life.

It's not just a matter of what you see. When I was working on the Boathouse Restaurant for Disney, I insisted on multiple elements, such as Amphicars, 27 unique and beautiful boats on display, an Italian water taxi, a gift shop (the Boatique), captains performing hourly bugle calls, and a complete line of rubber ducks for sale.

Layering is taking an idea that was terrific unto itself and adding to it, making it appeal to more people.

Layering is all around us. A man who's well-dressed is well-layered. Just on the torso, he can be wearing a T-shirt, button down, cuff links, tie and pin, sweater, sport coat, pocket square, and scarf over a coat and gloves.

When a chef serves a plate, he or she is layering. The plate is the canvas. The food is arranged in a way that is pleasing to the eye as well as to senses of smell, touch, taste, and feel. It helps evolve the dish and makes a memorable dining experience that motivates people to come back again and again. Layering and attention to detail create a unique experience every time. I can't tell you how many people have come to our laboratories and said to us, "I didn't see that last time I was here." Well, guess what? It was here, but your brain and eyes often don't work quickly enough to absorb all the different layers. On every visit to our labs, guests see something new.

All this raises the question: how much layering is enough? For me, it's a minimum of three elements. For instance, in a restaurant, you might start with the three basic layers of lighting, visual attractions, and sound. From there, of course, you can—and should—add on additional layers! That's because there's never really a defined endpoint to layering. Creative entrepreneurs never stop layering because they are always coming up with innovative ways to present ideas differently.

Layering and multitasking go hand in hand, in part because both are skills and passions that all successful entrepreneurs possess. And, like multitasking, layering can be a target of criticism from others. For them, enough is enough. What's the point of continually adding layers to something that's perfectly good? Leave well enough alone!

As an artist who utilizes the creations of other artists for my concepts, I see through different lenses. When Rainforest Cafe was first created, I added live birds in hopes of educating guests and the public about deforestation. Our education program was very successful because many guests would spread awareness by word of mouth. This was crucial for our PR and marketing.

When Rainforest Cafe was sold, the live birds were taken out of the restaurants because they cost a hundred thousand dollars a year for curators, food, and upkeep—an expense I felt was necessary for the concept. Getting rid of the beautiful, colorful, and engaging birds that symbolized Rainforest Cafe was unfortunate. The educational and engaging experience the birds provided guests was priceless.

Don't be afraid to release the inner child in you and give yourself the freedom of adding to and improving your project. Think, imagine, allow your mind to roam free, and revel in this amazing world where boundaries are limitless and anything is possible.

Conceive, Believe, Achieve

Entrepreneurs work in an essential three-step process: conceive, believe, achieve. And I believe that conceiving, believing, and achieving are intertwined with layering.

First, don't worry about constraints: *conceive*. Try to keep it simple. There will be plenty of time to add various layers to your ideas once you come up with them.

Next, believe in what you're doing. Many potentially successful entrepreneurs fail because they lack the necessary belief in themselves to push forward with their products or discoveries. As we have seen earlier, all the passion in the world is wasted if a person lacks the ambition to bring his or her creation out into the open.

Many decades ago, a famous clergyman and author, Norman Vincent Peale, wrote an optimistic book extolling the virtues of a positive mind-set, appropriately titled *The Power of Positive Thinking*. When all is said and done, the book's main thesis can be boiled down to one basic principle, both simple and profound: if you believe, you can succeed.

It is critical for entrepreneurs to believe in themselves and what they are doing. As we saw in Chapter 1, this is because the very nature of the entrepreneurial life comes with risk, failure, and a hearty portion of skeptics ready to dismiss your ideas. Because the essence of entrepreneurism is innovation and change, the entrepreneur must often challenge or change the status quo.

Stability and familiarity are comforting conditions for most people. Entrepreneurs have no such comforts; their challenge is to create new things, often in the face of fierce opposition from those who cannot grasp what they are doing. That's what I meant by emphasizing the importance of layering to an entrepreneur—challenging the status quo mandates change, and layering is at the very heart of change.

Consider an observation made by Henry Ford, one of the world's greatest entrepreneurs: "If you think that you can or you think that you can't . . . either way, you're right." That strikes at the core of the value of belief. And part of having the belief in your ultimate success lies with valuing the importance of layering.

If you're still having trouble believing in yourself, think about the words of Walter D. Wintle, who reminds us, correctly, that "it's all in the state of mind":

If you think you are beaten, you are
If you think you dare not, you don't,
If you like to win, but you think you can't
It is almost certain you won't.

If you think you'll lose, you're lost
For out of the world we find,
Success begins with a fellow's will—
It's all in the state of mind.
Full many a race is lost

Ere even a step is run
And many a coward falls
Ere even his work's begun.

Think big, and your deeds will grow;
Think small, and you'll fall behind
Think that you can and you will—
It's all in the state of mind.

If you think you are outclassed, you are
You've got to think high to rise,
You've got to be sure of yourself before
You can ever win a prize.

Life's battles don't always go
To the stronger or faster man,
But sooner or later the man who wins
Is the man who thinks he can!

Now step back and think for a moment. Did the artist who created that poem get it right the first time out? Not likely! He changed, revised, added, and subtracted—in other words, continued to layer what he had started out with. Layering makes any form of creativity a process that rewards passion and enthusiasm with the very best outcome possible.

The process of layering never really stops, but there does come a point when you need to prepare yourself and your creation for the marketplace. Let's take some time to focus on the product you've layered so carefully and diligently.

SECTION II

PRODUCT

CHAPTER 7

Be Excellent or Be Gone

There are no shortcuts to any place worth going.

—Anonymous

Self-Examination Question:

Are you willing to take the extra time and effort necessary to create a product or service that is excellent rather than acceptable?

Because creating themed restaurants and attractions is what I do for a living, I tend to be a self-appointed critic when visiting other eating establishments. Whether it involves the quality of the food or the overall ambiance of the place, I'm always on the lookout for ways to enhance the dining experience. This can sometimes create unintended consequences, a few quite memorable in scope.

Several years ago, I was visiting Japan and stopped at a famous Tokyo restaurant. In my never-ending quest for gustatory excellence, I challenged a veteran sushi chef on the freshness of his product. (The fact that it was my first visit to Japan and the chef was only inches away from my body holding an extremely large, sharp knife in his hand didn't deter me from voicing my culinary opinion when the sushi simply wasn't up to par.) Though the chef defended his product that day, a Japanese friend later told me the chef admitted to a colleague that the sushi was, in fact, a day old.

I suspect the average customer at that Tokyo restaurant wouldn't have noticed the sushi's lack of freshness, but that's not the point. It's all about excellence and giving your best, even if you might get away with doing less. Is getting away with less really worth it? Your work is a reflection of yourself, so why would you want a mirror of mediocrity?

Ever since my earliest days as an entrepreneur, I've been guided by two quotes that I had framed and placed on the wall over my desk:

"When you're out of quality, you're out of business."
"The noblest search is the search for excellence."

Aspiring and practicing entrepreneurs take note: if you keep these two thoughts and use them as guiding principles in your journey, your chances of reaching a successful destination will be greatly enhanced.

Just the other day, our senior vice president of retail asked me to review a new website for the Boathouse Restaurant. It featured attractive, artistic photos of the food set against the backdrop of the restaurant.

"Isn't that excellent? Doesn't that look good?" she asked.

I said, "Well, you see the back of the heads of the servers; you don't see their faces. And in some of the pictures, all I see is food and an empty restaurant. I would like every shot that has food in it, whenever possible, to be filled with people having a good time and enjoying their meal."

I didn't stop there.

"When you're shooting a picture of the restaurant, make sure the front entrance looks busy and in high demand, with people walking and talking. We don't want an empty shot of the front of the building. Some think that adding diners distracts from the image, but an empty restaurant looks cold and uninviting."

This also circles back to my advice to always trust your gut. If you feel something is not quite up to par, that something falls short of being excellent, pay attention to it. I don't confront people or get in sushi chefs' faces or send associates back to reshoot photos just for fun; I do it to make something go from good to great.

Ultimately, my approach to pursuing and maintaining excellence boils down to a simple turn of phrase:

"Be excellent or be gone."

That's a powerful statement and one that I embrace wholeheartedly. If you can't excel at something of importance, it's better to focus on something else where you can achieve excellence. Believe me: your clients and customers will notice the difference, and you will as well.

CHAPTER 8

Sweat the Small Stuff: Paying Attention to Details

The details are not the details. They make the design.

—Charles Eames

Self-Examination Question:

Do you believe that it's often the little things that make a big difference between success and failure in business?

There's an old saying that "the devil's in the details." I believe that's where excellence resides.

Conrad Hilton, famous for the chain of high-end hotels that bears his name, was a man who knew this concept well. To make sure the quality of his establishments remained high, Conrad would make regular announced visits to his properties to check things out. The story is that if, upon arriving at one of his hotels, he noted there was a lightbulb burned out in the lobby, he'd book himself a room for an extra day or two. The reason? If, knowing that the big boss was coming, the staff had still failed to replace burned-out lightbulbs properly, Hilton wondered what else might be amiss at the hotel. The burned-out bulb was the canary in the coal mine suggesting that service standards might be lagging. Maybe there were no problems and the lightbulb issue was a false alarm, but it was worth an extra day or two of the busy corporate executive's time to verify that things were right and service was up to Hilton standards.

Hilton understood it's the small things, added up, that determine the overall quality of an organization. Therefore, attention to detail was absolutely essential to obtaining and maintaining great customer service, the metric by which this hotel icon measured organizational excellence.

People often fail to realize just how important attention to detail is, both in business and in one's personal life. People who don't sweat the small stuff can lose some big stuff (as in big bucks), as was the case with the man who made a minor typing error in selling a bottle of Allsopp's Arctic Ale on eBay. The problem was he spelled it "Allsops"—a mistake that resulted in only two bids and a sale price of $304. When the winning bidder turned around and relisted the bottle on eBay, this time with the correct spelling, the listing generated 157 bidders and a sale price of $503,300! A half-million-dollar difference—that's gotta sting. (It's not confirmed that the bidder actually paid the $503,300, but wine experts believe the rare bottle of ale is worth at least five figures.)

One of the reasons I have had a successful relationship building themed restaurants for Disney is because the company likes our extreme attention to detail. I consider this the ultimate compliment because Disney's excellence is built on attention to detail. Go to any Disney theme park and watch the staff (particularly the executives) as they walk through the property. If they see a piece of paper on the ground, they'll stop and pick it up.

They sweat the small stuff. That's how they got to be big stuff.

In developing projects, my team and I focus on details to get things right in all aspects of our operations. It is advice I give and follow *rigorously*. Sometimes I'll miss a detail, and I'm always thankful when someone brings the oversight to my attention.

I remember one example in particular. It involved our Winter Wonderland restaurant concept, specifically the model railroad trains that run on elevated tracks around the display we constructed. One business associate, when touring our facility, noted that the locomotive pulling the string of freight cars had no smoke coming out of its stack. I looked closer, and, sure enough, there was a smokestack but no smoke.

I don't know how I missed it! I even remember as a kid having to put capsules in the engine of my own model train to create the smoke. Once the mistake was pointed out to me, I saw that the effect of the train simply wasn't the same without it. Maybe it seems like a small thing to you, but to me, my omission was a step backward from excellence; it compromised the quality of what we were trying to create. It was a problem that needed fixing.

If you're really paying attention to details, you can pre-solve problems before they have an opportunity to occur. In our renovation of the Green Acres Event Center (see more in Chapter 29), I kept the original materials and charm of the barn while adding all the modern conveniences of a brand-new event facility. The reason was that, in researching similar venues, I found that many guests who had attended events at barns often left early because it was too hot, cold, windy, humid, buggy, or smelly. They were uncomfortable, and we learned so many people had bad experiences at barns due to the weather and lack of modern amenities.

We didn't allow that to happen. Central heat and air conditioning were added. After some doing, so were city sewer and water lines. (The only way to make this happen was to go under a two-lane highway and connect to a nearby airport's sewer system.)

We didn't stop there. We added handicap-accessible bathrooms, an elevator, and outdoor ramps. We installed thousands of lights. More than fifty chandeliers were placed throughout the barn, all equipped with dimmers to create just the right mood and ambiance. At the beginning, we watched clients bring their own sound systems—which were terrible. Music is so important to the atmosphere and enjoyment of an event, and we wanted to raise the bar by improving the music quality at Green Acres Event Center. So we decided to add an audio setup that played music throughout the entire inside and outside of the barn. We also wired the facility to accommodate a twelve-piece band.

The details go beyond the right equipment and setting. When reviewing emails, memos, marketing copy, and other written materials, we read them out loud. The reason is that you can often hear something odd that doesn't stand out visually. It's another way to focus on the details, the nuances that make a big difference.

We also sweat the small stuff when it comes to outreach. The first thing we did in 2018 was update our contact list. I must have had a hundred people on my list whose information had changed or who had, sadly, passed away. We called every single contact on the list—upward of seven hundred people—to update his or her profile. We got birthdays and spouses' names; we found out whether they had children.

Updating this information was a lot of work, but, as getting rid of something that's no longer useful is just as important an element of paying attention to detail as is adding new information. As a matter of fact, I'm just as happy throwing things away every single day as I am buying new things. It allows me to see clearly and focus on the details.

Of course, it's not easy to stay focused on the small stuff, particularly since many entrepreneurs see themselves as "big-picture thinkers." The truly successful entrepreneur has to have what has been called the "helicopter view": the ability to gain enough mental altitude to see the big picture while retaining the ability to descend, hover, and see the details, too. You need to think big but also focus small.

This past year, I was bringing a client into the office for a tour. I noticed a cigarette butt on the walkway right in front of our door. I don't know how long it had been there, but I stopped, bent down, and picked it up. The client was amazed. In his eyes, he saw a menial task, something most executives would ignore or leave for others to do. "I'm not sure I would have even spotted that cigarette butt, let alone picked it up," he said. He then added, "If you take that much pride in the appearance of your property and have the eye to spot small imperfections, it probably reflects on the quality of what I'm about to see."

Little things.

Sweating the small stuff.

People notice. They see you care passionately and appreciate your attention to detail. It helps turn them into loyal clients, customers, and investors.

Noticing the small stuff can also enhance the marketing and presentation of your product. I think back to early architectural renderings of the interior design for the restaurant Backfire BBQ. We had an incredible team working on the concept, but when I got the designs, they just looked wrong. It took me a few minutes to figure out what was missing: the architects had forgotten to add any people, so the restaurant looked totally dead. The bar was simply deserted. We wanted, of course, to portray a bustling restaurant full of people, food, and energy—a venue that looked like the place to be, not a place that was just hit by the plague.

When I pointed out this problem to my architects, one of the partners told me, "You know, in twenty-five years, nobody has ever pointed out what you just spotted. It really makes sense."

Attention to detail: it makes a difference.

Excellent detail-oriented service is what can transform a passerby into a loyal customer. And when investors notice, it's all the better.

Sweat the small stuff. It'll help you earn the big stuff!

CHAPTER 9

Always Be on the Lookout for Your Next Big Thing

I'm here to build something for the long term. Anything else is a distraction.

—Mark Zuckerberg

Self-Examination Question:

As you observe the world around you, do you make an effort to ask yourself: "Is there something here I could create (a service or product) that would be beneficial and could be monetized?"

As a young boy I was always on the lookout for products or services that people need.

Opportunities are waiting for you to find them! It is amazing how many exist when you get in the habit of looking for them. It's just a matter of training yourself to automatically scan your environment for what I call "enhancement gaps"—places where improvement could be beneficial.

My first chance to use this principle occurred at just thirteen years old. During summers, I worked as one of several cabana boys at the Silver Gull Beach Club in Breezy Point, New York. My official duty was to get the cabanas ready for use by putting the chairs and umbrellas out each morning and then clearing everything away in the evening. It was simple, straightforward, and not very demanding.

During my first week on the job, I noticed there was a group of adult men who played cards around some makeshift tables near the swimming pool. Sometimes, one of the men would call me over to run an errand for him, such as getting him a sandwich or some extra ice for his drink. For this service, I would get a tip, sometimes as much as ten dollars. So I started hanging around the card players more often, and, sure enough, once the guys saw me there on a consistent basis, they started asking me to run more errands and do more favors. Hot towels, cold towels, pastrami sandwiches, umbrellas, sunglasses, it didn't matter. I never failed to honor a request.

I was making a hell of a lot more money being their gofer than I was as a cabana boy, as I'd generally score a five-dollar tip for my efforts. If any of "my" card players wanted something, I made sure they got it. I became known as the go-to guy for anything. One time, a player got a flat tire in the parking lot. He told me to take care of it, and I had it repaired within an hour. I never said no to any request. I had become a card-table concierge and was being paid handsomely for my services.

The longer I watched the game, the more I realized there was a treasure trove of additional money that could be made. For example, I noted that some guys would fight for certain seats at the table (usually their "lucky" chair or a spot in the sun), so I started reserving their favorite chairs for them. Of course, the players showed their gratitude by giving me generous tips. I used my tip money to purchase new tables and chairs and charged a "rental" fee to play. The men paid me a five-dollar sit-down fee. What had started as a one-table game expanded, under my direction, to a three-table game. It became a card room, and all the players were happy because I was giving them what they wanted: an upgraded playing environment and someone to run errands for them when they didn't want to get distracted from the game. I was turning a tidy profit and providing needed services at the same time.

There was more. I noticed that the guys could use up to seven packs of cards a day during their play. With three tables, that meant twenty-one packs of cards were needed to keep the action going. I decided I could make extra money if I supplied the cards directly to the players rather than having them purchase the decks for retail at the local drugstore. I found out the brand of the cards and located the manufacturer's distribution point, which turned out to be in Far Rockaway, three bus rides away from the club. Every week, I would make the trip to the distribution point and buy several cases of brand-new cards. Because I bought in bulk at wholesale prices, I was able to mark up the decks 150 percent and still charge the players less for the cards than they would have paid at the local drugstore. Plus, I saved them the trip to the store in the process.

The games were played only on Saturdays and Sundays, yet I found myself making about seven hundred dollars a weekend based on card sales, table rentals, and tips garnered from running errands. Meanwhile, none of the other cabana boys had any idea about the kind of money I was raking in.

The following summer, I added additional money-making wrinkles to my card table operation. I purchased a refrigerator, stuck it out near the tables with an extension cord, and stocked it with iced tea, lemonade, and orange juice—I even tried to slip in some vodka (without success, as I was still only fourteen). I started selling the drinks directly to the players, keeping both the markup on the beverages and the tips I got for bringing them to the tables. I got to know each player's favorite drink and made sure I had enough stock to never run out. Every time I brought a drink to the table, it was another five bucks in my pocket, plus the profit margin I made between my cost for the refreshments and the markup I charged the player.

I even concocted an idea for saving money on ice. In the early days of my operation, I used to pay for bags of ice from a nearby convenience store and haul them to the club. Then I realized it would be cheaper (and by that I mean *free*) and less hassle to just take ice from the kitchen at night when no one was around and use it to keep the drinks cold. I also started running errands for the *families* of the players, tapping into yet another income stream. The players started asking me to deliver drinks to their wives, and they'd tip me for doing so. The guys even began betting on how fast I could run a given errand. I usually made money on that wager, too. The cash was rolling in at an extraordinary rate.

Sadly, it was around this time that I made my major mistake: I started bragging to my cousin about how much money I was making. He had worked at the club for five years as a cabana boy, and when he heard about my seven-hundred-dollar weekends, he bounced off the wall. "Seven hundred dollars for two days' work?" he said with disbelief. "You've gotta be kidding me!" He spread the news around, bragging as a very proud relative about my business acumen.

It was a very short time later that the general manager pulled me into his office. He was nice about it, but he made it clear my gravy days were at an end.

"You make more money than I do," he said. "I've been in business a hell of a long time, and you're one hell of an entrepreneur. We love you and want you to stay on and be part of our team, but we're taking over the card tables."

I, of course, wanted no part of it. I had built the business through my purchasing skills, sweat equity, and great service. Now the club wanted to take over what I had created. When I didn't accept the club's offer, the manager hired one guy and two girls to do what I had done by myself.

My card table business days were over. But the lesson I learned would last a lifetime: observing your surroundings to see what you can do to make things better is a surefire formula for turning a profit. This is what entrepreneurism is all about. It's about spotting a need that isn't being fulfilled then acting quickly to create a product or service to meet that need.

If something ignites your passion, pursue it. It doesn't necessarily have to be immediately financially profitable. Follow it, enjoy the experience, and savor the feeling of being fully engaged.

This is what I experienced with the cute water/land vehicles called Amphicars. From the moment I saw them, they became an obsession. I acquired and learned about these retro cars before introducing them to Disney for the Boathouse Restaurant. After years of research and development (R&D), they are now enormously successful from a financial standpoint. (You can read more about the venture in Chapter 30.)

Enhancement doesn't necessarily have to involve something that's completely new in and of itself. The Amphicars are not new, as they were built in 1961, but they were novel and greatly enhanced a preexisting setting. That's another element of enhancement—taking something that already exists and making it better by layering. Like layering, enhancement means never being completely satisfied with something as it is. Keep looking for ways to improve it and make it more exciting.

Earlier, I shared the importance of lighting at Green Acres Barn Event Center. Thanks to the development of LED lighting, we were able to manipulate the mood at the facility by adding lighting to the exterior of the barn. A wide spectrum of color options, from red to blue to purple, enhances the uniqueness of the venue. Ten years back, this technological opportunity for venues like Green Acres did not exist.

I never stop looking for enhancement opportunities. The first version of this book was used as an elaborate business card. We used the book to travel around the country and speak. We also placed the book in Rainforest Cafe, T-REX, Yak & Yeti, and the Boathouse. Not only were we able to sell more books that way but also we were able to use the income generated to support our varied philanthropic interests. Opportunities are endless.

Go forth and spot some enhancement gaps. They're out there just waiting to be exploited. Your next financially profitable idea, product, or service might be no farther away than something you observe the next time you walk out your front door.

CHAPTER 10

Research and Development: Learn It If You Want to Earn It

I believe in innovation and that the way you get innovation is you fund research and you learn the basic facts.

—Bill Gates

Self-Examination Question:

Are you willing to invest your own money, even when it is costly, to sufficiently fund the needed R&D to explore new ideas, products, and services?

When we opened our first T-REX restaurant in Kansas City, I was approached by a reporter who had just finished touring the facility. He had spent the better part of an hour looking at the animatronic dinosaurs, the prehistoric decor, the themed dining rooms with ice caves and meteor showers, the fossil dig, and the retail store. "How long did it take you to come up with all this?" he asked.

"Our team spent five years and fifteen million dollars working on the concept before we ever earned a dime," I replied.

The reporter was shocked that it cost so much in money and time to develop.

He's not alone. Many people underestimate the amount of research and development that goes into bringing a successful concept, product, or service to market. One of the biggest mistakes many restaurant owners make is underestimating how much time and money in R&D they need to make their concept a success. They also don't like to spend the needed time and money up front in researching and developing the best way to achieve excellent results. They want to get to the marketplace quickly and at minimal cost so they can start showing a return on investment (ROI). Sadly, such an attitude can cost more than it saves.

One advantage of R&D is to uncover, before too much time and money are wasted, which undertakings are viable and which ones are not. I have found that more focused attention on R&D will greatly enhance the chances for success. The extensive R&D that my team and I undertook in developing Rainforest Cafe, T-REX, Yak & Yeti, and the Boathouse, was a major reason for their success. It was through years and years of painstaking study of the Rainforest Cafe concept that I came up with my "11 Commandments" for making a themed restaurant profitable. These are the foundations of the development process.

My 11 Commandments for Successful Themed Restaurants:

1. **Entertainment:** We strive to create an immersive environment that is an entertaining escape.
2. **Education:** Our interactive themed environment stimulates the desire to learn.
3. **Environment:** We genuinely care about what is happening to our planet and constantly look for ways to improve it.
4. **Employees:** Our employees help us be the best that we can be. We are only as good as the people around us.
5. **Earnings:** Return on investment (or, in Schussler Creative terms, return on *innovation*) makes our projects viable.
6. **Sight:** Visual stimulation keeps our guests connected and engaged. They eat with their eyes first.
7. **Sound:** We use music as an easy, inexpensive way to enhance the atmosphere.
8. **Smell:** Each customer's sense of smell is immediately excited by the aromas of great food to be enjoyed.
9. **Touch:** The textures of the interior, ranging from soft and luxurious to glossy and futuristic, should complement the food and atmosphere.
10. **Taste:** Dining at our restaurant is a delicious and memorable experience. If it tastes great on the palate, then it will be great for the profit.
11. **Passion:** Passion is our driving force for creating and improving the customer's experience.

To get a better idea of how successful our products and services will be in the marketplace, we hire focus groups to test our ideas. For example, when we were designing T-REX, we brought in groups of kids to test the viability of our retail offerings and "fossil dig"—an archaeological sandpit where they could unearth dinosaur bones and other prehistoric treasures. Through that experience, we learned exactly where the kids liked to spend the most time and planned accordingly.

Because of the amount of time and effort you will need to commit to a project to ensure its quality and success, it's important that you are passionate about your idea and submerge yourself in it fully. This often involves investing a lot of time networking with experts, going to museums, traveling, and researching in libraries. In general, the bigger the project is, the more time you'll need to spend learning about it, essentially becoming an expert in that field.

Part of the thrill of being an entrepreneur is the education I receive along the way. Take T-REX as an example. I didn't know anything about dinosaurs until I spent countless hours researching them. As I was poring through every bit of information I could find, I learned that dinosaurs had feathers with vibrant colors and various patterns. When I was a kid, we were taught that dinosaurs were brown, black, and green monsters. Bright, colorful feathers make them more incredible than we ever imagined!

The learning process hasn't stopped there. We're still experimenting with our animatronic dinosaurs: How long will the dinosaurs' skins last? What is the impact of UV rays on the skins? What kind of upkeep will be required to keep our mechanical models operational? Quality research and development are never-ending.

We're now in the heart of researching five new concepts for Disney. Thanks to the passion and energy we devote to R&D, each concept is bursting with potential.

T-Rex, A Prehistoric Family Adventure™—A Place to Eat, Shop, Explore and Discover™, Steven's fourth restaurant at Walt Disney World Resort in Orlando, Florida.

While the ice cave inside of T-REX at Downtown Disney in Orlando, Florida, features a T-Rex skeleton frozen in the wall, the restaurant is kept at a comfortable room temperature for a cool dining experience. The ice cave changes color during the meteor shower shows that happen every 20 minutes within the restaurant.

There are some rules that I'd like to suggest with regard to R&D. First, don't expect everything to work out. That's simply not possible. In fact, part of the process of R&D is identifying those things that work and those that don't. Rather than becoming discouraged when an idea simply doesn't fly, be glad that your research revealed that. You can now direct your energy and resources toward something with far greater promise.

Additionally, don't limit R&D to your comfort zone. Research and development give you the opportunity to stretch yourself and your ideas, so don't be shy about exploring radically different projects and concepts. You may discover that even if you are not a huge fan of an idea, others may fall head over heels for it. R&D will reveal new insights and can help you identify those things that will engage others far more than they might engage you.

Enjoy the ride. R&D is a voyage of discovery, an opportunity to learn. Absorb yourself in the process and joy of discovering new ideas and concepts.

Lastly, dive into R&D to the level that makes the most sense to you. When I'm developing an idea, there are some people who ask me why I don't just do an architectural diagram. Why do I go through the extra effort and build three-dimensional vignettes of what I'm trying to create? It's simple. I'm better able to sell my ideas when people are able to see the details built out into a tangible form and experience them with all five senses. When investors, potential partners, and operators see the time and financial commitment that it takes to build and maintain these living, breathing, life-size models, they know how dedicated I am to delivering an excellent and entertaining product and experience.

It's certainly more work and more expensive, but it's well worth it. Without R&D, you can't possibly do your best in creating and marketing your product and service. Research and development is the most direct route to that destination called excellence.

CHAPTER 11

Make Improvements—Before and After

The biggest room in the world is the room for improvement.

—Helmut Schmidt

Self-Examination Question:

Once your creation is in the marketplace, do you still look for ways to improve it?

I have encountered many entrepreneurs who rush their products or services to market too quickly. There are numerous reasons for the haste, including the need to recoup costs, meet investor or company deadlines, make a living—or simply the urge to see one's creation come to fruition. Great ideas, like great wines, need proper aging: time to bring out their full flavor and quality. Rushing the creative process can lead to results that are acceptable for the market but below the standard of excellence that could have been achieved had the entrepreneur taken additional time to let the ideas fully ripen.

The creative process is not a cut-and-dried scientific equation. No one can give you a mathematical formula that will reveal with certainty exactly when your idea has reached that perfect moment of maturity to harvest. For most innovative people, that point is instinctive. There is an inner sense of knowing when the time is right. However, this feeling is very fragile and can be easily disrupted or distorted by pressure to get to market more quickly.

Most entrepreneurs don't have the luxury of limitless deadlines and unlimited funds. Thus, they must strike a balance between allowing their ideas ample time to mature while still meeting the demands of their backers and sustaining a living. My hope is you'll do your best to give your ideas time to breathe and not push forward so quickly that you short-circuit your creative process.

In my career, I've certainly seen how giving the creative process breathing space can transform a product from acceptable to exceptional.

Several years ago, I set out to create a themed restaurant that served up an incredible barbecue menu and featured motorcycles, cars, and jukeboxes, with energetic and colorful neon signs. I decided to call the concept America's Roadhouse. After letting the idea incubate for a while, I decided the restaurant didn't have enough of an "action" look, so I had my architectural firm do a second rendering with a *Dukes of Hazard* feel. But it just wasn't there yet.

Left to right: Mikey Teutul, Paul Teutul Jr., Steven, and Paul Teutul Sr. visiting the Orange County Choppers headquarters in Newburgh, New York, during the early development of the Backfire BBQ restaurant.

I decided I didn't like the "peanuts on the floor, hot rod out the door" look . . . it needed something more.

At about this time, I became fascinated with a new cable show, *American Choppers*, which focused on a father and his sons who created and ran the custom motorcycle business Orange County Choppers. I thought it would be great to feature this concept in my new restaurant. The OCC theme seemed to go better with a more art deco, sleek, hip look, which would appeal to young and old patrons alike. So I contacted Paul Teutul Sr., and the OCC concept became part of Backfire BBQ: Bikes, Burgers, and BBQ. It featured a great menu and highlighted the stars of the television show, along with the Orange County Choppers motorcycle insignia, on the front of the restaurant.

At each step, I could have decided the restaurant was good enough and finalized the design. Yet, by not making a snap decision, by allowing enough time to let the creative process work, by being willing to make improvements when the OCC opportunity presented itself, and, finally, by getting other creative people involved and competing to present the best possible product, we were able to create a themed-restaurant concept that was far superior to the original.

This comes back to the concept of layering that I discussed in Chapter 6. Layering takes many forms, and no one says you absolutely have to have two, three, or four layers. That's entirely up to you. When I created Rainforest Cafe, I had honeysuckle and grapevines. I had animatronic animals—gorillas and exotic birds, all placed at varying levels in the ceiling. Then I had the greenery for the canopy of a tropical rainforest. Never once did it occur to me that enough was enough.

It's also important to encourage others to give feedback. This saved me from a huge blunder during the marketing of T-REX. As an opening-day gimmick, I thought it would be clever to have a huge animatronic T-Rex placed right outside the entrance to the restaurant. We'd program it to pick up a child (a paid actor) in its mouth, transport him over a low wall separating the establishment from the parking lot, and deposit him at the restaurant's front door. My staff was *horrified* at the idea and rightfully pointed out what I had inexplicably overlooked: that five hundred kids waiting in line to eat would probably run away hysterically, never to be coaxed back again!

Making Improvements after Marketing Your Product or Service

I have an entrepreneurial friend who once told me, "Steve, once my product is out there for public consumption, I'm done with it. It's time to move on." It's disheartening to see that many entrepreneurs share his belief: create it, sell it, and forget about it.

It is sound business practice to evaluate products and/or services you create once they've been on the market for a while. It is often the case that glitches and problems with specific products and services become apparent only *after* they are in the marketplace. This is where unanticipated difficulties and unexpected results can arise. What matters is how you react to them.

In 2006, we opened the Yak & Yeti restaurant at Disney's Animal Kingdom. A family-friendly, Asian-inspired restaurant, it was divided into two parts: a sit-down indoor area and an outdoor walk-up window. One of the advertised benefits of the walk-up window was faster service.

Several months after Yak & Yeti opened, I stopped by to see how things were going. I took a seat outside, near the "quick-service" outdoor section of the restaurant, and noticed people having to wait in line for up to fifteen minutes to place their food orders. This was a huge problem with an obvious solution.

The placement of the menu boards caused a long delay for customers making their food selections. The only menus available were behind the serving counter, so the patrons had to wait in line until they got close enough to the counter to read the menu. This gave them little time to make their choices. When they reached the counter, they weren't ready to make their selections. As the employee behind the counter waited patiently for the customers to make up their minds, the lines grew. The solution was simple: additional menu boards had to be posted along the sidewalk where the customers lined up. That way, people positioned at the back of the line would have more time to make their decisions and, when they got to the front of the line, would be ready to place their order without further delay, speeding up the process significantly.

How do you ensure that you are delivering what is expected of the product? I have often visited the same place a hundred times, and then something catches my attention on the last visit that I missed before.

Remember: whether it involves making improvements before or after you market your product or service, you should never stop assessing, enhancing, and learning all you can.

Keep improving! Stay in the game of change. It is going to happen with or without you, so you might as well embrace it.

CHAPTER 12

On Marketing: Customers Won't Buy What They Don't Know Exists

Good marketing makes the company look smart.
Great marketing makes the customer feel smart.

—Joe Chernov

Self-Examination Question:

Is marketing a significant part of your entrepreneurial plan?

One of my friends is a writer. At the first writing of this book, his manuscript had just been accepted by a New York publisher. Nine months after it was accepted, the book hit the stores. In an attempt to boost sales, the publisher's marketing department asked my friend to do some interviews and bookstore appearances. He refused, claiming that it was "beneath [his] dignity" to "peddle [his] work." As far as he was concerned, his job was to write the book and the publisher's job was to sell it.

Obviously, marketing was not a priority for him. Maybe if you're a John Grisham or a J. K. Rowling, you can get away with birthing your book and then letting others raise it to marketplace success, but the majority of entrepreneurs and independent contractors do their own work. Taking a personal role in marketing your product effectively is sometimes as important to the success of the product as creating it.

I never, ever miss an opportunity to market my creations. Success or failure is determined not solely by the quality of what you produce or provide but also by public awareness.

Early in my career, I received a call from a magazine writer who wanted to do a feature story on our new themed restaurant, JukeBox Saturday Night. I jumped at the chance for the publicity. Actually, I *flew* at the chance. I hopped on a plane from Chicago to Los Angeles the very next day to meet with the journalist who wanted to interview me. I ended up with a major article on my restaurant appearing in *Entrepreneur* magazine. As a matter of fact, it became the cover story. Would that have happened if I simply did a phone interview from Chicago and didn't fly out to Los Angeles?

Probably not.

What if I hadn't responded to the writer at all?

What a loss of valuable publicity.

There are many who have commented that I spend as much of my creative energy figuring out how to market our ideas as I do creating them. I don't think that's true, but I certainly recognize the importance of marketing for achieving success, and so should you. Of course, some entrepreneurial undertakings are more easily marketable than others. But I believe almost any product can be marketed if the entrepreneur uses his or her imagination and will expend effort to gain public awareness and media attention.

When I was running the Minneapolis location of JukeBox Saturday Night, I was always thinking up publicity stunts to bring more business to the club. Before the Minnesota Twins made it to the World Series in 1987, I offered to clean each fan's "Homer Hanky" (which fans twirled over their heads during the game) outside my establishment. I arranged with the owner of the dry-cleaning service across the street to set up a row of washing machines outside JukeBox, where we created an assembly-line cleaning process. Thousands of fans got their hankies cleaned and pressed. They loved it. It created a lot of goodwill. Of course, a lot of the fans, proudly sporting their spotless hankies, then stepped into our restaurant, spent money, and swelled our bottom line. On top of that, we got free extensive radio, television, and domestic and international newspaper coverage—far more publicity for our establishment than we ever could have afforded with our limited advertising budget.

When the Twins made it to the World Series, the city allowed me to close off the street in front of JukeBox Saturday Night for pep rallies, complete with banners draped across the street. Coincidentally, the Shrine Circus was in Minneapolis—and that gave me another idea. I asked myself: What bigger impact could I possibly bring to the rally and also market the fact that the circus was in town? After developing a strategic partnership with the circus, we arranged for elephants to parade down the closed-off street, with city officials riding on them and leading the crowd in singing "Take Me out to the Ballgame." It was a win for everyone involved.

After the Twins won the World Series, we got another shot at a marketing coup. Paul Ridgeway, the big-time event planner in charge of organizing the victory parade, called me and said, "I heard you're from New York and wondered what kind of parade a Manhattan guy would throw." I suggested a ticker-tape parade—an idea he accepted and quickly put me in charge of. So I planned the ticker-tape parade but with a twist: the ticker tape wouldn't be paper confetti; it would be real money, millions of dollars of shredded U.S. currency!

Everyone jumped on board with the idea. Now all I had to do was get the money: ten million dollars' worth, to be precise. I checked with several local banks, the FBI, and even the CIA. They thought it was the craziest idea they ever heard but directed me to the Federal Reserve Bank in Minnesota. The people there were much more positive about the plan. They had to take old money out of circulation and destroy it anyway, so it wasn't much of a stretch to chop the cash into confetti-size pieces and send boxes of the stuff in a Federal Reserve truck directly to my restaurant. The Federal Reserve Bank didn't charge us a cent, as they loved the Twins, too. We tossed all the confetti-cash into a rented dumpster and announced we were giving away millions of shredded dollars in the parade. People began lining up at seven o'clock in the morning and waited hours for a chance to scoop up free money into paper bags. We gave out mounds of cash to thousands of families. The PR we got was worth well over a million dollars: the story of the "confetti-cash" ticker-tape parade made the front pages of both *USA Today* and *The New York Times*.

The confetti-cash parade demonstrates how marketing your product can be profitable and fun: JukeBox got a bottom-line boost from the event, and everyone had a good time in the process. (Well, *almost* everyone. It turns out that the Federal Reserve banking system got thousands of additional requests for "confetti-cash" after our parade, and the institution vowed never to give out shredded money again. From what I understand, it has kept that promise to this day.)

Steven in front of Jukebox Saturday Night Club in Minneapolis, Minnesota, relishing the $10 million dollars of shredded money that he persuaded the Minnesota Federal Reserve to give away. The mountain of cash confetti, weighing in at 2,000 pounds, was used for the ticker-tape parade celebrating the Minnesota Twins World Series Championship of 1987.

As far as I'm concerned, the boundaries of my marketing efforts are limited only by my imagination. I always challenge myself to find new and impactful ways to attract attention to my product and make the process fun. You can, too. Once you incorporate the marketing function of your product or service into your overall plan, you'll find yourself getting more enthusiastic and excited about generating publicity.

My passion for marketing has led to some wild and crazy stunts. One time, I was slated to address a gathering of reporters and business leaders about the advantages of Backfire BBQ, our Orange County Choppers–themed restaurant. Everyone was seated in a large tent near the proposed construction site. When it was my turn to speak, heads turned and people stared as I came roaring in on a hundred-decibel, custom-built motorcycle, wearing a fancy suit, shiny Italian loafers, and a big grin on my face. The photo of my entrance made all the newspapers and turned a humdrum conference into a media-worthy event.

For the groundbreaking of T-REX in Kansas City, we scheduled a few dignitaries with gold-plated shovels—the usual groundbreaking skit. I decided to spice things up. The night before the ceremony was to take place, we buried some replicas of dinosaur bones cut in the ground. The next day, with press gathered around, the chosen movers and shakers turned the earth with their gold shovels . . . and "discovered" dinosaur bones. Meanwhile, the mayor, who was sitting atop a backhoe, plunged the scoop into the ground and pulled out the huge T-Rex skull. Everyone laughed, and the scene played out as the featured story on the evening news and the front page of the newspaper.

The day before Super Bowl Sunday in 2018—the year the game was played in Minneapolis—my phone rang at ten o'clock in the morning. A gentleman named Morris Goldfarb, who heads one of the top clothing representatives in the world was calling.

"I've got Macy's executives with me, and they would like to see your laboratories and your offices," he said. "I was wondering if you would allow us to come by."

I called my staff, but nobody wanted to work the day before Super Bowl Sunday. I tried to explain how important it was to be reactive, to be available, and what a great opportunity this might be. But no one agreed, and it wasn't just because of an impending big game. As one of my associates pointed out, it takes hours just to set up a tour of the laboratories: "Steve, we want to put our best foot forward. We don't want to do something that isn't up to our standards."

Then it occurred to me that I didn't have to show them all my laboratories; I could take them through just one. I called my associates back, told them we could do that with time to spare, and they agreed. Instead of taking up the whole day, we were done in a couple of hours. And, just as important, we hit it out of the ballpark. They all were blown away by our concept. We were grateful for the chance to create new friends and relationships that could lead to so many opportunities.

The bottom line is, in marketing, you need to learn how to react fast, with enthusiasm and passion.

Bear in mind that marketing and public relations can also be dangerous and don't necessarily occur in a positive environment. Bad news about your business can hit television or the newspapers—in case of a disaster, you need to be ready with a plan that can be implemented immediately. Who's going to talk on the company's behalf? Do you have emergency contact numbers at the ready?

When you're successful, you attract attention—attention that demands having to raise the bar every single time.

One of the most successful and rewarding forms of marketing occurs when you take a negative and turn it into a positive. The Amphicars at Disney World are a perfect example. Those were often described as the worst car and boat ever built but the best toy ever.

Reengineered, now they're both fun and reliable. Look up Amphicars today, and what sort of picture do you see? A happy family having the time of their lives as an official-looking captain guides the car on a tour of Lake Buena Vista. You can't buy that kind of publicity.

Another marketing principle I always observe when trying to sell my ideas is that if the customers can't come to you, you go to them. For some entrepreneurs, this is simple and straightforward; they show up with a briefcase full of papers or a computer and PowerPoint presentation. With my creations, "presentation" takes on a whole new meaning.

When we first began pitching our T-REX concept, we were interested in selling it to the Simon Property Group. The executives were not able to visit our laboratory in Golden Valley, Minnesota, but they were willing to see what we had to offer if we came to their headquarters, located on the upper floors of the Hyatt Hotel in downtown Indianapolis, Indiana. The question was: How could we effectively get them to fully experience and appreciate our concept?

The answer: a floor show.

I met with the general manager of the Hyatt Hotel, and he agreed to my plan, which included unloading four twenty-eight-foot semitrucks packed with mechanical dinosaurs and associated props inside his lobby. The entire area was to be transformed into a prehistoric jungle. The whole job had to be completed between six o'clock in the evening and six o'clock the next morning. Because the dinosaurs were so big, we couldn't simply cart them in the front door. We had to hire a team of employees from a glass company to pull the plate-glass windows out of the front of the hotel so we could fit the dinos into the hotel lobby—and then put the glass back in place. The glass-removal process had to be repeated when we were ready to pack up and leave. It was quite a scene, with a row of glass-company trucks stacked up outside the Hyatt and a bunch of guys pulling out windows and hauling dinosaurs into the lobby of the hotel. It cost us thirty-five thousand dollars to get this show set up.

The next morning, the executives of Simon Property Group walked through the lobby I'd transformed into a jungle, and they were blown away. They had never seen such a creative sales presentation. We ended up with a deal.

Another time, we rented a convoy of trucks and headed to Orlando to show Disney our T-REX concept. This was an even bigger effort than the Indianapolis trip. We had dozens of dinos ready for showing. Our enthusiasm was over the top, but our timing was unfortunate. I was on a plane heading to Florida to give my presentation on September 11, 2001. In flight, we got the news of the attack on the World Trade Center in New York. The plane had to make an emergency landing. When I finally arrived in Orlando, nobody was in any kind of mood to see a presentation. It was a sad day for us but a far sadder day for our country.

It was at this point that David Siegel stepped in and changed the mood. David is a wonderful friend and leading time-share developer based in Florida. He was gracious enough to give us permission to set up our display for a week in the ballroom of his Westgate Resort, about five miles from Disney. What started as a weeklong occupancy ended up as an eight-month odyssey. It took that long to get the Disney people, still reeling from one of the most devastating events in the history of our country, to check out our project and get on board with the idea.

Marketing your product or service can be a fun challenge, and I never miss an opportunity to present our ideas. For that reason, I used to carry a working model of T-REX in the back of my car. The model was about four feet by four feet and cost thousands of dollars to build. But it was there when I needed it, always available for a spontaneous showing. I remember many a lunch or dinner with a potential investor where the topic of the restaurant would come up and the investor would say, "I'd really like to see that someday." I'd smile and, at the end of the meal, lead the person out to my car, pop the trunk, and—presto!—a portable T-REX concept.

I never stop selling our ideas. I'm always thinking of new ways to promote what we're doing. If someone wants to see my projects, I want to be ready to go on with the show . . . because it might be the only chance I get to pitch that investor. That means I'm always ready with multiple ways to market my ideas. You should be, too.

CHAPTER 13

Make Your Budget "A Sophisticated Guide"

A budget is telling your money where to go instead of wondering where it went.

—DAVE RAMSEY

Self-Examination Question:

Do you give enough attention to staying within project budgets? And, if you go over, do you have a suitable explanation?

Entrepreneurs and budgets don't always mix.

I define a budget as "a sophisticated guide." That's something many investors don't want to hear because they want to know specifically what a project is going to cost.

Understandably, budget overruns can create tension between entrepreneurs and their backers. The best way to handle budget problems is to keep an open line of communication throughout the project. It is essential that the investor and entrepreneur are on the same page when it comes to understanding what a project will cost and how the money will be allocated. Have those important conversations about vision early. And make sure you have them often throughout the project.

Budget overruns occur all the time and often for very valid reasons. A great example is the Boathouse Restaurant at Disney in Orlando. For five years, they said no to this project. Through dogged persistence and maintaining great relationships, they gave us the opportunity at Disney Springs. It took us a year and a half to build. What was originally supposed to cost $18–$20 million wound up running up to about $28 million. That's a substantial budget increase!

The overruns were unavoidable, but there were many solid reasons for them. First of all, there's the "Disney factor," which always adds 15 to 20 percent to a project. This high standard of excellence is always expensive to achieve, and that was explained early on to my investors. Then add the fact that the building had to be built three-quarters over water. Not only did we have to use galvanized steel to protect against rust but Disney is so strict about safety that we had to put sprinklers underneath the deck that was right over the water—seemingly redundant but necessary. We also built a five-thousand-square-foot kitchen, which is one of the largest on Disney property.

The timing and logistics of the project also proved costly. Barges were needed to work on the water. We had to work at night so as not to disturb the restaurants and stores with construction noise during business hours. All cars and trucks related to the project had to be off the site by 8:30 in the morning so that stores could open nearby without mess or clutter.

True, it was a budget overrun, but the result was a restaurant that was so much more than it might have been.

There are two essential strategies to address the possibility of budget overruns. First, build in a contingency amount that's greater than you anticipate the project will actually cost. If you give yourself a 30 or 40 percent contingency, you have a cushion. Instead of surprising investors by going back to the well and asking for money at the end of a project, you can return money and tell them you were under budget.

Second, stay in constant communication with your investors. Make them aware of your contingency plans at the beginning of the project and, should you exceed your budget, be ready to explain in detail why it occurred *as it occurs*, not just at the conclusion when you present them with the bill.

Budgie vs. Budget

One problem entrepreneurs have when it comes to budget considerations is the clash between what they think must be spent to make their idea work and the amount of money the investors believe is sufficient to bring the project to market. For example, one of the main attractions of the original Rainforest Cafes—and a major reason I built them—was to highlight the beautiful parrots that inhabit the real rain forests of the world. My love affair with these creatures began when I was a teenager. At 18, I got my first scarlet macaw, named Jules (after my father), who is still alive and lives with me to this day. I felt that these beautiful creatures would not only add to the authenticity of the rain forest dining experience but also encourage people to appreciate the birds and help promote their preservation around the world.

Keeping the birds in each restaurant was not cheap. Before we came along, no tropical birds had been allowed around food for reasons of food safety. To get permission to put them in the restaurant, I ended up working with health department officials—both local and federal—to invent a specialized air filtration and purification system. That cost money. So did the eight-hundred-square-foot habitat room where the birds were kept when not on display in the restaurant. Then there was the cost of feeding the birds and paying trained people (a curator with several assistants) to look after the birds' health and welfare. All in all, it cost about one hundred thousand dollars per year to keep the birds in each Rainforest Cafe.

When the Rainforest Cafe chain was sold to Landry's in 2000, it was decided that, when it came to birds versus bucks, the parrots were an excessive cost, and they were removed from the restaurants. Of course, I didn't agree with that decision. I felt the marketing value of the birds alone justified their cost, but I was overruled. As an entrepreneur—unless you cover all the costs to create, market, and sell your own product or service—you need to recognize that those who foot the bill for bringing your product or service to market have some say in how and where that money should be spent. *How* much say they have should be clearly spelled out in advance of going forward with any business deal to avoid hard feelings and, worse, potential legal challenges down the road.

Drove My Chevy to the Levee, but the Levee Was High

I have come to believe that there will always be some budget tension between creative entrepreneurs who want to present their perfect innovative vision and pragmatic business investors who want to get the highest return on their investment. Back in my JukeBox Saturday Night days, I had wanted to find a 1957 Chevy to cut in half, using the front end to stick outside the building, with it actually coming out the front wall. I told my partner, Jimmy Rittenberg, about the idea and said it would cost a few grand to buy the car.

Jimmy said, "A few grand? Why not buy a '50 Ford and cut it up? You can get one of those for nine hundred bucks."

I replied, "It's not the same."

He argued, "What do you mean, 'It's not the same'? It's the front end of a car."

I countered, "It's not the front end of a '57 Chevy. The '57 Chevy exemplifies the fifties and sixties, what we're trying to create here. When you look at a '57 Chevy, the car smiles at you. When you look at a '50 Ford, it says, 'Screw you.'

I finally got the money, but it was a tense and uncomfortable situation. Beauty is in the eye of the beholder. Creative decisions are not always reached by consensus.

You're Welcome!

One of my most memorable experiences with going over budget happened during the construction of our first Rainforest Cafe at the Mall of America with Lyle Berman, the venture capitalist who backed the project from the outset.

At the time, the restaurant was close to completion, which was the good news. The bad news was that I was a million dollars over budget. When I called Lyle to tell him, he was—to put it lightly—unhappy. "How can you be 50 percent over budget?" he asked, a question I sensed he didn't really want answered, because he didn't wait for a reply.

"Listen, Steve," he said, inhaling sharply. "I want you to take the rest of the day off and enjoy yourself. Have you seen the movie *Bugsy*?"

"No," I replied.

"Well, I want you to promise me you'll go rent a copy and watch it tonight."

"Why that movie?" I asked.

"Just do it," Lyle answered and hung up the phone.

That evening, I watched the film . . . and promptly got the message. For those of you who haven't seen the movie, Benjamin Siegel, the main character in the film, is murdered for going over budget building his lavish Las Vegas casino. Of course, Lyle was joking (I hope), but I was much more careful about coming in at or near budget from that point on!

No one's proud to stand up and raise his or her hand to say he or she was over budget. But a budget overrun is not an overrun when it pays for itself and then some. If you had pinched pennies and "stayed" on budget, would the eventual results have been the same?

There's an interesting epilogue to the Mall of America Rainforest Cafe story. Yes, I was some $1 million over budget and, yes, my partner, Lyle, was very upset. But, at the time the project was being developed, I had forecast that we would do about $4.5 million in sales in the first year.

As it turned out, we grossed $14 million.

I wonder whether Bugsy Siegel's budget-obsessed partners would have cut him a bit of slack if they knew just how much money that casino would eventually pull in thanks to his "fatal" overrun.

CHAPTER 14

Don't Be Afraid to Develop Strategic Partnerships

The power of one, if fearless and focused, is formidable, but the power of many working together is better.

—Gloria Macapagal Arroyo

Self-Examination Question:

Do you consider strategic partnerships to further your success?

One time, when I asked a group of students to pick some words or phrases they thought described entrepreneurs, one of the common responses was "lone wolf." It is an apt label, as many entrepreneurs do choose to work alone, to toil independently in search of a product or service that will bring them financial success. To a certain degree, the magnitude of a project will be a factor in how easy it is to go it alone in bringing that product or service to market. But for projects big or small, what an entrepreneur should avoid doing is reinventing the wheel.

It is a waste of time and resources to undertake this duplication of effort, and, often, the wheel that is already out there is better than the one the entrepreneur can create. This is where the development of strategic partnerships comes into play.

Here is a case in point. All of our restaurants have a retail component, a store within that sells products related to the theme of the restaurant. Our T-REX chain of restaurants is no exception, and, when first developing it, we decided plush dinosaur toys would be a great product in its retail stores. Young visitors at the restaurant could build their own dinosaurs from a selection of various prehistoric animals in attractive colors, outfits, and accessories. In fact, an existing company called Build-A-Bear Workshop did a great job with bears. It was successfully operating in malls throughout America.

We could have attempted to duplicate what Build-A-Bear had already achieved—but why? They had an excellent product, so why spend time re-creating what was already available? We decided it was smarter to join forces with a business that already offered a superior product than to spend unnecessary time and money trying to prove that we could do the same thing. Build-A-Bear had already researched the product, had the factories and the means to produce what was needed, and had an established reputation as a great retailer and promoter.

I cold-called Maxine Clark, the dynamic brains behind Build-A-Bear, and suggested a strategic alliance between our companies.

She agreed to visit my laboratories in Minnesota with her executive team. Maxine loved the idea and agreed to spend half a million dollars to retool her operation so she could create a Build-A-Dino retail outlet in our T-REX establishments. It was an instant success at T-REX. Both of our companies profited from the partnership. Approximately 25 percent of our total sales comes from our retail operations, and 50 percent of all retail sales comes from one product: Build-A-Dino. The partnership with Maxine Clark's Build-A-Bear is a win-win and a classic example of avoiding duplication of effort, saving time, enhancing marketing potential, and making profit for all concerned.

The Build-A-Dino example also underscores the importance of maintaining close ties with your strategic partners. Maxine has since retired from Build-A-Bear, and Sharon Price John has assumed her role. I called her to introduce myself and mistakenly assumed that Sharon would naturally know who I was and know about my partnership with Build-A-Bear. It took numerous calls, and I had to explain my entire history and relationship with Maxine to a new assistant in hopes of reaching Sharon. Because I had not stayed in touch to maintain my relationship, it took a lot of effort to finally connect with her.

I was embarrassed that I didn't even know Maxine was retiring. It was a lesson for me about the value of staying close to your strategic partners.

This falls in line with some words of wisdom by Harvey MacKay, author of seven best sellers. Mackay advises that the contacts in your Rolodex are the most important tool on your desk. In his book *Swim with the Sharks without Being Eaten Alive*, he cites the Mackay 66 Customer Profile, a sixty-six-question document that enables you to build and maintain a comprehensive record of every client, customer, and partner. In addition to the usual details—name, birthday—the profile includes information about whether a customer attended college (and if not, is he or she sensitive about it?), the interests of

Steven with a great friend, mentor, and New York Times best-selling author, Harvey MacKay during a visit to the Hot Dog Hall of Fame prototype in Golden Valley, Minnesota.

a customer's children, and even the names of people the customer seems intent on impressing. It's that complete!

I've had many unique partnerships, including an agreement involving Budweiser and Royal Crown Cola. I got the local Budweiser distributor to help sponsor construction of a giant mural depicting King Kong climbing the wall of our JukeBox Saturday Night in Minneapolis. The artwork included a real Cessna 150 airplane coming out of the wall and an actual helicopter parked on the roof of the building directly over our front entrance. The chimney of the building became the Budweiser beer can that King Kong was holding.

This mural was so popular with the city and the public that we later convinced the family that owned an adjacent building across the parking lot to allow our mural artist to paint a second rendering of the Wizard of Oz. It was Royal Crown Cola International, manufacturers of RC Cola, who sponsored that mural.

There was an outdoor space between the King Kong mural on our building and the Wizard of Oz mural on the building across the parking lot. We did not own that space, but—given the popularity of both pieces of artwork—we often got permission from the city to stage outdoor events for hundreds of people in that area. What an advantage, as it increased the volume of customers we served, positively impacting the bottom line.

The benefits of strategic relationship building are multilevel. Those murals and our strategic relationships with the vendors and our neighbors spanned seven successful years. We ended up with an eye-catching gimmick that generated publicity and profits for JukeBox. When was the last time you heard of a soda company and a beer company working together?

With creative thinking, you can come up with strategic partnerships to enhance the creation of a product or service, improve its quality, promote marketing and public relations, and boost your profit margin. Lone wolves have often achieved entrepreneurial success. But ask yourself: is there a well-vetted pack that you should join to take your product or service further?

CHAPTER 15

Marketing Yourself to Market Your Product

Self-Examination Question:

Do you consider (and take advantage of) the impact you have when selling your idea, product, or service?

Many years ago I agreed to attend a Broadway show with a friend from New York. I don't remember the name of the show, but I vividly recall my friend's reaction when he discovered the actor in the lead role was sick and would be replaced by an understudy.

"Let's get out of here," he said firmly.

"Why?" I protested. "We already paid for the tickets, and we've got good seats."

"I came to see the actor who is sick."

"But the show's still going on," I said. "Besides, the understudy might be just as good."

My friend was resolute. "I came here to see the main actor, not some backup," he huffed. "I don't want to see the play without him." And with that, he got up, motioned me to follow, and walked out of the theater.

Now, here's what I find interesting: there are many venture capitalists and investors who feel about entrepreneurs the way my friend felt about the actor in the play—they don't want to go on with the show unless it's with the specific entrepreneur in whom they have invested. The person committing his or her money to a project is as concerned (or more concerned) with who is heading up the project as he or she is with the project itself.

For this reason, it is critically important for aspiring and established entrepreneurs to keep in mind that success in convincing investors to back your project will always be based on two things: (1) their perceived viability of your idea and (2) their impression of you. In other words, when it comes to entrepreneurial success, you need to be able to sell your product or service and be able to sell yourself as well.

Think about it. If someone came up to you and said, "Will you back me with cold, hard cash?" what factors would you consider in making your decision? You would assess the commercial value of what the entrepreneur was proposing, but you wouldn't stop there.

You'd also be interested in that person's commitment to the idea, his or her sense of dedication to the proposal, and the "sweat equity" he or she was willing to invest in making that dream a reality.

Now, I'm not suggesting that all entrepreneurs have to go so far as turn their houses into rain forests or load up warehouses full of dinosaurs to show investors they are committed to their idea. But immersing yourself in your concept or idea certainly tells a potential investor you're committed to achieving your objective. After all, investors are risking their money on you; they want to know you have something at stake as well.

"How committed are you to your idea?" I can't tell you how often investors have asked me this question. After seeing my rain forest house, some investors thought I should be committed—not to my idea but to an institution! But when they saw what I was willing to do to make my idea work, they were impressed. They saw the raw ambition, passion, and enthusiasm. They saw my level of commitment, and it gave them a reason to invest. When someone shows true passion and enthusiasm for an idea, it makes people want to be part of the vision. It convinces them that the idea will succeed and that their financial investment will reap significant dividends.

If you don't believe strongly in your idea, who else will? If you don't show enthusiasm and dedication to your idea, why would anyone else get excited about its chances for ultimate success? If you don't stand behind your idea with a commitment to labor vigorously to see it become reality, what kind of person will offer financial backing to see it through to completion?

Investors want you to have skin in the game.

Go out there and sell your idea, or your product, or your service, but don't forget: you also need to sell yourself. How strongly do I feel about this? Strongly enough to unequivocally state that promotion is a central focus of my life? I believe that the day you stop promoting yourself is the day you die.

Making a Good First Impression Is Critical

In a perfect world, new entrepreneurs going out with their first idea would make just one appointment with a venture capitalist who would immediately agree to provide the funding needed to make the idea a reality. If only it were so! Seasoned entrepreneurs, even the successful ones, know that rejections and desperate scrambles for financial resources are the rule rather than the exception in the contemporary business world.

It's tough to get people to give you their money, but you can increase your chances of success if you present yourself to potential investors in the appropriate manner. You need to behave and dress in a manner that will enhance your credibility and, in turn, increase the probability that an investor will take you seriously enough to consider risking money on your idea. This is particularly important the first time you meet a prospective investor, because first impressions are often lasting impressions and color any interactions that follow.

Behavioral scientists have identified things you can do to make a positive impression on people you want to influence, focusing on such things as dress and nonverbal behaviors to enhance your interpersonal success with others. Some techniques work better than others. I used to assume that any thinking individual would practice these techniques because they were common sense. Sadly, common sense doesn't always translate into common practice, and I am amazed at how many otherwise intelligent and creative individuals fail to practice the most rudimentary steps in establishing a good first impression. Add to this the fact that many articles and books have been written on the topic of establishing good first impressions and it becomes even more astounding that would-be entrepreneurs don't follow established and well-known procedures for impressing potential clients. Thus, I find it necessary to mention these recommendations for making a positive first impression. They really do make a difference in gaining the confidence and cash of clients whom you look to for support of your project.

Physical Appearance

There's an old saying that "clothes make the man." (In today's world, we would want to include women in that statement and recognize that it is still as valid today as when it was first spoken.) I always make it a practice to wear a suit or sports coat when I'm meeting with investors or attending business meetings where my projects are discussed. That includes visits to Florida, where people often say I'm overdressed because it's hot in the Sunshine State and many people just wear collared shirts at work.

I don't agree with them. I think a polished jacket is mandatory apparel for a first meeting with a customer, client, and/or investor. When I visited the Disney Imagineering Department, I wore a suit. I felt it showed respect for the people I was meeting. It's a bit like the newscaster who told me why he wore makeup to cover up the dark circles under his eyes when he was on the set. "I'm in people's living rooms for a half hour or more," he said. "I owe it to them to look my best." He's got a point. I don't think you can be too overdressed, but you can end up underdressed. Why take the risk?

Physical appearance also involves the way you groom yourself, even the way you smell. It does no good to wear a carefully crafted suit or dress and then show up with hair coming out of your ears and nose. Dirty hair and unkempt beards are also a no-no, along with scraggly nails, bad breath, body odor, or the use of too much cologne or perfume.

The Handshake

The handshake is a critical part of most first meetings with potential investors. If you do it incorrectly, it might be the only time it happens.

If you do it right, it increases the chances you'll shake hands again when you close your deal.

Nobody likes a wet handshake. It turns people off. If you have sweaty palms, make certain you wipe them off so they're dry before you attempt to shake hands. Never grab the end of someone's hand, as it can be perceived as offensive. Limp hands tell the person you do not care. The grip should be firm, but it shouldn't be bone-crushing; it is not a wrestling match. Additionally, pay attention to the length of the shake, and take care not to shake too long. It's a handshake, after all, not a finger embrace.

Body Language

Joe Navarro, highly respected body-language expert and coauthor of *What Every BODY Is Saying: An Ex-FBI Agent's Guide to Speed-Reading People,* points out that 60–70 percent of all communication is nonverbal. With those kinds of numbers, you can see why physical gestures play a critical role in determining the overall success of your interactions with others. You need to be aware of the body language you are giving off for others to see. Your facial expressions are particularly critical. Looking indifferent, hostile, or displeased will not sit well with someone you want to impress. Don't roll your eyes, sneer, tighten your jaw, or compress your lips. These nonverbal behaviors will often be interpreted negatively by the person who sees them. A display of friendliness, a well-timed smile, and appropriate eye contact (not too long but made on a regular basis during a meeting) will create a more positive atmosphere, as will good posture (alert and upright, not slouching or leaning away) and attentiveness (looking all over the room sends a message of disinterest and will not be well received).

Try to remain calm and interested throughout your meeting. Pay attention to what your potential investor has to say; don't constantly interrupt or give short replies to his or her questions. Listening carefully not only shows respect for the speaker but also will allow you to gain a better understanding of what he or she wants. Bobbing your head up and down gently while the other person speaks and/or tilting your head to one side also facilitates communication and sends out a nonverbal message that you have a receptive attitude toward what is being said.

Leave Something That People Will Remember You By

Each time I meet a new person, that individual could be a potential investor or someone who might provide assistance in some way. Sometimes these meetings are planned, like when a person visits my laboratory for a tour; but often they're not, like a chance encounter with a businessperson assigned to the seat next to mine on a cross-country flight. At the end of these interactions, I always want to leave the person with something special that will make me memorable in his or her mind. I want to give the person something that will help jog his or her memory about who I am, should I need to call or work with him or her sometime in the future. I want the person to have something that represents me as a creative entrepreneur and sets me apart from all the other business contacts people make in their lifetimes.

What might that something be?

An item that few people think about, but that I have developed as a major marketing tool in my entrepreneurial endeavors, is the business card.

The business card. It's either the first or last thing you give to people when meeting them. It's also the item by which you are remembered, should the person who received the card have reason to use it in the future.

I created my first unique business card in the mid-1980s, a plastic card in the shape of a 1957 Chevy convertible. When I first came up with the idea for the card, my partners thought I was crazy. Each card cost twenty-five cents, a huge chunk of change in those days. But it was made of plastic, so it was indestructible—you could spill drinks on it and you could bend it, but you couldn't break it. Every JukeBox Saturday Night I owned at that time had a '57 Chevy sticking out the front wall, and I drove a restored '57 Chevy, so it turned out that the item was more than just a business card; it was a reflection of my personality. In fact, my business card *was* me.

The card ended up generating far more publicity and attention for our club than it cost to produce. The card was featured in *Inc.* magazine and *The Detroit News*, and people still keep the card even though the club has been closed for decades. Business card collectors called me to acquire them, and quite often I would get calls from guests requesting "one of those cool business cards."

I have continued to create unique business cards as a way of setting myself and my business apart from the competition with each new themed attraction, restaurant, and retail store we open. I'm always working to develop a card that makes a person say "WOW!" when he or she receives it. I figure if we claim to be innovative and creative, then our cards better reflect that claim.

I have spent hundreds of hours and gone through dozens of card designs before settling on a card I'm satisfied with. Sometimes the type is too small; sometimes the logo seems wrong or the colors aren't perfect. Sometimes the card is too large or too small or the shape isn't quite right. But, eventually, I am able to produce a business card that captures who I am as a person, what our team is as a company, and what makes us special. The cards are expensive, but people don't forget us when they receive one. Oftentimes, they will put the card in a prominent place and refer to it in conversations with others.

As an entrepreneur, you might want to consider designing a special business card to capture the attention of your prospective investors. I would also recommend that you develop a telephone answering system that is memorable and unique so that when people call your business, they don't get dead air or canned music but rather learn innovative, useful information about what you can do, are doing, or have done. The important thing is to set yourself apart from the crowd and to give people something by which to remember you. (See Chapter 24 for more on this subject.)

The recorded voice on your telephone message should be upbeat and infectious. Having an engaging voice is sometimes as important as the content of the message. Produce an effective phone message and you'll be giving yourself a valuable entrepreneurial edge over your competition.

There are a few crucial moments in setting impressions, so it's essential to be aware of each of those make-or-break opportunities. By taking care in the way you present yourself and your business to others, you can effectively set the tone and tenor for a potential investor's entire opinion of you. It's essential to always remember that the critical first impression can often be what seals the deal.

SECTION III

PERSISTENCE

CHAPTER 16

Persist and Prevail

A diamond is a lump of coal that stuck with it.

—Anonymous

Self-Examination Question:

Do you give up easily, or are you willing to pursue your goals with tenacity and determination?

Many of us dream, yet few of us achieve our dreams. Why? Sadly, it is often because we give up too easily. We accept one setback as total defeat and break off our pursuit of a goal because we lack the mental toughness to keep going. If only we had the determination to stay the course, to persist in our quest for success. One man had such a dream, and he lived to realize it because he dedicated his life to realizing it. Consider what he went through.

He failed in business in 1831.
He was defeated for the legislature in 1832.
He had a second business bankruptcy in 1833.
He suffered a nervous breakdown in 1836.
He was defeated for speaker of the Illinois house in 1838.
He was defeated for elector of the Illinois senate in 1840.
He was defeated for the U.S. Congress in 1843.
He was again defeated for the U.S. Congress in 1848.
He was defeated for the U.S. Senate in 1855.
He was defeated for the U.S. vice presidency in 1856.
He was defeated a second time for the U.S. Senate in 1858.
He was elected president of the United States of America in 1860.

Would you have had the persistence to stay the course after taking so many risks and failing so many times? Not many people would. But, as Abraham Lincoln found out, persistence pays. A century after Lincoln's inauguration, baseball great Tommy Lasorda would elegantly describe what "Honest Abe" had discovered: "The difference between the impossible and the possible lies in a person's determination."

In my own life, I've always been a "never say die" kind of guy. If I took on a task, I never wanted to quit until I achieved my objective. I always believed that if I tried hard enough and long enough, I'd prevail. I remember back in high school my coach once sent me into a basketball game to try to stop the opposing team's highest scorer, who was just killing us. I wasn't much of a basketball player since I was too short, but I could jump high for rebounds. And what I lacked in height I made up for in tenacity.

I remember hounding my opponent at every move. I was in his face, bound and determined that he wouldn't get the ball or, if he did, that he wouldn't get a clear shot no matter what. I was *determined* to keep him from scoring. I was like a bulldog, the annoying, relentless kind that doesn't let you move anywhere without being on your case.

I guess my opponent wasn't used to being guarded by someone with such a fierce desire to do his job with persistence. He got so mad that he threw the ball at me and got kicked out of the game for unsportsmanlike conduct. Mind you, I never fouled the guy or did anything illegal; I just persisted with all my energy—and when a person persists with all his or her heart, that person usually gets results.

When I was in radio and television sales, I utilized the persist-and-prevail philosophy to get jobs. I already mentioned my Superman story as one example in Chapter 1. I'd like to add one additional comment about that experience here, as it has to do with perseverance in the face of potential failure. At several points during my trip to the station manager's office, things went wrong, and I could have become discouraged while jammed into that crate and just climbed out and scuttled the plan. I guess you could call it my "Kryptonite Moment." I could have succumbed. But I didn't. I persisted. I played the hand I was dealt. I didn't give up. Even when faced with potential humiliation—stinking of rancid meat, hair matted with Diet Coke, my Superman outfit stained with particles of salami and pickle—I went on with the show.

When the lid came off that barrel, I could have stood up and apologized, asked for a doctor, and slunk off in embarrassment. But that isn't my style. Life isn't always scripted. You have to play with what you have, go with the flow. At the end of the day, those who succeed are those who are flexible, who can adapt to unanticipated circumstances, and who even turn unexpected situations to their advantage. What's most important is that they are capable of persisting in the face of adversity.

I learned that lesson well when my superhero persistence earned me a job offer. And it was a lesson I recalled when it was time to find my next position.

I wanted to be in television sales, so I contacted a top agency in New York City and decided to send the chairman of the board my résumé in a manner that would catch his attention. I purchased a huge toy boat—one about four feet long with three smokestacks and that looked like a passenger cruise ship. (This was not the kind of vessel you'd play with in the bathtub; there'd be no room for any water.)

I put my résumé in the boat, put the boat in a large box, and had it shipped to the chairman via special delivery. I figured that it would be the first résumé he ever received that arrived in a boat. Along with the résumé, I enclosed a letter that concluded with "Please welcome me aboard."

About a week later, I got the boat back in the mail along with my résumé and a reply that said, "Your boat has leaks in it, but keep trying."

Well, needless to say, those words were just the challenge a persistent person loves to hear. I purchased some miniature life preservers, attached them to the boat along with my résumé and a new letter, and shipped the whole thing back to the chairman. The letter said, "I'm your life preserver. Welcome me aboard and your boat will float again."

That got me a plane ticket to New York, an interview, and the job.

I was determined when it came to romance, too. Once I'd met the girl I wanted to marry and was ready to pop the question, I wanted the best chance of getting an affirmative response, so I decided to create a romantic setting with a little help from my friends in Florida. I rented out the Magic Kingdom at Walt Disney World (yes, the entire park) and put my plan into action.

Just before the park officially closed to the public for the night, my girlfriend, at the time, and I were eating dinner at one of Disney's restaurants when the waiter (who was in on the scheme) told me I had an important call. When I left the table to take the call (there were no cell phones in those days), a Disney character, dressed as Major Domo, approached my girlfriend and said, "Please follow me." She hesitated but did as she was told, walking out to the street where a coachman, dressed in tights, a wig, and a tricorn hat, stood next to Cinderella's lavishly decorated carriage, pulled by twelve white horses.

Major Domo told my girlfriend to get in the carriage. While she tried to figure out exactly what was happening, the coachman drove her through the entire Magic Kingdom. Even though the park was now closed, all the lights remained on, and music was playing everywhere. The coachman pulled alongside the Cinderella Castle and stopped. Major Domo helped my date step down from her seat, and there, against the backdrop of the castle, stood Mickey, Minnie, Donald, and all the other Disney characters, lined up waiting to greet her. A six-piece band was playing in the background.

At that moment, from the other end of Main Street, I came to my "princess" astride a large white stallion. I was dressed in a Prince Charming outfit and carried a glass slipper in one hand. I rode up to my lady, dismounted, and, bowing down on one knee, carefully placed the slipper on her foot (it fit!) and took a ring from my pocket.

That's when I asked her to marry me. Fortunately, she said yes, and the moment the words came out of her mouth, the sky lit up with a prolonged burst of fireworks.

Persistence, with the proper stagecraft, can do wonders for entrepreneurial romance.

On a more serious note, I cannot emphasize strongly enough how important it is for you, as an entrepreneur, to keep the faith and stay the course. I think of the twenty-six times I pitched Rainforest Cafe to Lyle Berman without success before getting his support on my twenty-seventh try. What would have happened if I stopped at twenty-six?

Of course, there are some times when throwing in the towel is not only the wisest course of action but also the only appropriate response. Nobody can afford to throw good money after bad forever; we all have physical, financial, and temporal limits. However, I do believe many entrepreneurs give up too easily; they walk away when things are not hopeless.

With Lyle, from the very beginning, I could tell he was interested in what I was doing, just not interested enough to commit to the project . . . yet. His response was the kind of reaction I call the "conditional no." It is a no but not a *total* no—an "I'm leaving the door open" kind of no. Those are the kinds of responses I'm looking for when I feel that persistence will prevail. As long as there's a sliver of interest in what I'm asking for then I'm going to keep pushing until I'm convinced that any further efforts will be futile.

Persist and prevail. The history books are full of famous, successful people who made their way to the winner's circle because they kept trying: Disney, Walton, Hilton. They had bulldog determination to reach their goals.

Do you know how many thousands of people went through our T-REX concept in more than five years without making a deal? Nobody does R&D for five years. Nobody spends fourteen or fifteen million dollars on a laboratory in a suburb of Minneapolis, filling warehouses with themed environments for restaurant and retail concepts. *Nobody.* It was a huge financial debt and a huge commitment

Donald Trump; Kiki the Cockatoo; Marla Maples, Trump's second wife; and Steven during the opening of Rainforest Cafe at Downtown Disney in Orlando, Florida.

Donald Trump and Steven at the Downtown Disney Rainforest Cafe opening.

of time and personnel. But we believed that it's impossible to put the time, money, energy, passion, and commitment into something and not have it work. We persisted until we succeeded.

Bulldog determination isn't easy. As Newt Gingrich once observed, "Perseverance is the hard work you do after you get tired of doing the hard work you already did." I can relate to that. It's not easy persisting when that elusive goal is still not reached. But persist you must. The apple highest on the tree always leaves the sweetest taste.

CHAPTER 17

"No" Is "Yes" Waiting to Happen

There are two ways to say yes:
right away or after I change your mind.

—Anonymous

Self-Examination Question:

Are you the kind of person who will make a concentrated effort to convince somebody that he or she might have made the wrong decision?

In a perfect world, the word "no" wouldn't exist. It wouldn't even be in the dictionary. Every request you made would be granted. It would be like that smiling loan manager at the car dealership with the sign on his or her desk: "We love to say yes."

But the entrepreneurial game isn't a perfect world. In fact, I strongly suspect that the vast majority of entrepreneurs have to endure an ocean of noes before getting to the Island of Yes. That's the way it is when you're asking other people to do you favors or lend you money or approve your plan.

Because no is the contemporary entrepreneur's constant companion, one has to learn how to deal with it and what steps to take to change no to yes.

Reacting to No

Having the right attitude when it comes to hearing no is critical for the entrepreneur. It involves developing the correct reactions for coping with the word when rejection is cast in your direction:

1. *You can't be shocked or crushed when you hear the word "no" because you will hear it no matter how good you are.* I always steel myself for a no whenever I make an offer or ask for something from a client, customer, or investor. That is because most people, even if they like what you're offering, aren't likely to run up, pat you on the shoulder, and heap lavish praise on your efforts. Why should they? It puts them at a disadvantage in the negotiating department when it comes time to talk cold, hard cash. If you're buying a house, do you make your highest offer first? Unlikely. You point out problems; you might even feign disinterest. If you're selling a house, do you accept the first price tendered? Probably not. You might even act haughty and highly insulted. Coming to

an agreement is a process of give and take, and no is part of that process on the way to yes.

2. *You should think of no as a "four-letter word"—something you hate to hear and are loath to accept.* Frankly, what I detest most is someone saying I can't do something. It's almost like challenging me to a duel. I have a can-do attitude, and a can't-do response is like throwing down the gauntlet at my feet.

3. *You can't get discouraged and give up when the "no" word is uttered.* Don't let the weight of disappointment keep you from pursuing your dreams. Persistence and determination override rejection and disappointment.

4. *You need to believe you can change no into yes with the proper aptitude and effort.* Nothing will ever get done if you don't have a positive outlook on your project. Your projected attitude and passion show your confidence!

5. *You need to have faith in yourself and what you are trying to accomplish.* After all, if you don't believe in what you're doing, who will?

The Second No and the Conditional No

Unless things seem utterly hopeless, I always try to give a potential investor, client, or customer at least one chance to change his or her mind from no to yes. If that person says no a second time, I ask myself this critical question: *Was the no an emphatic no?* In other words, was it a solid rejection?

If it was a solid rejection, then I will probably look elsewhere (to another investor or client) for a favorable response. However, if the no was not *emphatic* but rather a *conditional no,* then I will keep trying until I sense the no has become emphatic. This is where your good judgment and experience play a major role in determining whether you persist or desist in dealing with an individual. Obviously, (a) the greater your belief in what you're selling, (b) the more important you perceive the person you are trying to convince to be, and (c) the greater your sense that the no is conditional and not emphatic, the longer and harder you should work to change no into yes.

Turning No into Yes

I make it a habit to handle a first rejection from a potential investor differently from a second rejection. The first time I get a no, I usually try to sweeten the offer or take some action that will lead to a yes the second time around. After all, as mentioned previously, most people don't start out saying yes the first time around; they need a little prodding and some negotiating room.

Early in my career, when I was selling Proctor & Gamble ad spots to TV stations in Chicago, I approached one account executive who represented several stations and made an offer she promptly refused. Of course, I was disappointed, but I wasn't ready to give up, either. I knew that a first no is only a final no if you stop asking. In this case, I got to be friends with the woman and discovered we shared something in common: we both wanted to try skydiving but hadn't done it. And so I arranged for a one-day skydiving course. We learned the ins and outs of skydiving during an all-morning lesson and then went for our actual skydive in the afternoon.

I remember the moment like it was yesterday. We were up at 3,500 feet, and the executive had agreed to jump first. As she was making final preparations for her big moment, I handed her a contract for ad time and said, "Just in case something happens, would you like to do something really nice before you jump?" She didn't sign, but at least she was smiling as she left the aircraft.

It was a long way down. Fortunately, we both enjoyed the jump, suffered no noticeable bruises, and, a few weeks later, she did sign the agreement.

The moral of the story? Sometimes you have to be prepared to go the extra mile (or jump the extra 3,500 feet, as the case may be) to get a no changed to a yes.

Because of my extraverted nature, I will often do crazy things to swing a no to a yes. When I was still selling TV advertising in Chicago, for example, I dealt with a buyer who wouldn't see me or even speak with me on the phone. When I found out that she worked in a windowed office on the sixth floor of a nearby building, I tried a more persuasive way to introduce myself: I rented a crane and had myself hoisted to a position right outside her window. When I rapped on the window, she looked up and saw me suspended sixty feet off the ground, holding a sign that read, "I'm Steve Schussler. Can I make an appointment to see you?"

That got me into her office the very next day. She said she thought what I did was funny and decided to see me because (and I am quoting her directly) "who knows what you'd do next had I said no." She made time for me, and I wound up with a deal. What's more, my antics caused a big buzz in the industry, which helped me get more business.

There was also the time I was trying to sell ad time to the vice president of marketing for the Coca-Cola Company. His name was Tom, and I could never get past his secretary to make my offer. I decided to get his attention, and hopefully some face time, by buying him a birthday cake and topping it off with candles I had purchased from a magic store—the kind that you can't blow out.

Cake in hand, I walked into the outer office where Tom worked and told the receptionist it was his birthday and I had this cake to deliver to him. "Oh my gosh," the receptionist gasped in surprise, likely mortified she hadn't known. "He's giving a speech right now in the auditorium. Would you like to present the cake to him there?"

I agreed, not realizing there were five hundred people sitting in the room.

Of course, no one except Tom and I knew that it wasn't really his birthday when I walked in, and everyone started singing "Happy Birthday." When I got on stage to give him the cake, he had some very choice words for me, including, but not limited to, swear words and death threats that only I could hear. He also asked who the hell I was. I told him and said I wanted to get his attention. Things got worse when he tried to blow out the trick candles and couldn't. But I ended up getting the order from him.

Of course, you can get in a lot of trouble pulling the kind of stunts I came up with to turn no into yes. It's all about timing, knowing how far you can or can't go with someone, and a bit of luck, too. In the case of Tom, I had heard he was a good sport, and, fortunately, my intel was good; otherwise, his non-birthday might have been my last birthday.

The point of these examples is not to turn you into a major prankster or even a minor trickster. Instead, they're meant to encourage you to find an approach that fits your aptitude and personality to get people to change from no to yes. The very bold approaches I used in these examples fit my personality at that time in my life and were geared to work with people whom I felt would appreciate that style of persistence. I believe they worked not just because they got attention but also because once people saw what I was willing to do to land the account, they started thinking, "Gee, if this is what he'll do just to *get* the account, think of what he'll be capable of doing once he *has* it." This strategy is what I like to affectionately refer to as "calculated crazy."

Again, doing humorous, outlandish, or crazy things to sell yourself or your ideas is certainly not the only or preferred approach for getting someone to go from no to yes. I used some of my own examples simply to demonstrate that using the right attitude and playing to your skill set can go a long way in changing a negative response to a positive outcome.

CHAPTER 18

Learn from Failure; Graduate to Success

The gem cannot be polished without friction,
nor man perfected without trials.

—CHINESE PROVERB

Self-Examination Question:

Can you experience failure and still retain the self-confidence necessary to seek success?

"Show me an entrepreneur who has never experienced failure and I'll show you a liar."

One of my early business partners made that claim more than thirty years ago. While there could be some exceptions to his rule, I doubt there are many. The very nature of the entrepreneurial life makes for a greater likelihood of failure. This is because true entrepreneurs are taking risks, trying new things, going places where no one else has ever been—and that entails the opportunity for great rewards but also the very real possibility of disappointment and failure.

Many entrepreneurs have experienced the highs and lows, the ups and downs, the successes and failures that come with the territory. I should know; I've taken a few major tumbles myself on the way to success. Here are just a couple that are worth pointing out.

Over many years, I dreamed up and created the concept of Winter Wonderland, a magical winter village complete with an indoor ice cave. Building this living, breathing model has cost a lot of time and money. One of the most expensive parts of the concept is the ice cave, which needs to be kept at 15 degrees year-round and constantly maintained as the ice disintegrates. Having this expensive prototype in my laboratory without a suitable destination where it could be effectively used is what some people would call a failure. I have been told many times to move on to a new idea and let this one go, but that is not in my nature. An inner voice drives me to push on and improve this concept.

Some of my most recent improvements include a train with a homemade wooden railroad track running through our office that visitors can ride and view our other concepts before ultimately ending up in Winter Wonderland. The train features small bench seats for passengers, a loud horn, and real steam billowing out of its smokestack.

Even with fifteen people putting in three and a half weeks of solid work, the first time we tried the train, it wouldn't go around the bend, and it fell off the tracks. Did we stop? By no means. We bought a second train so we could more closely examine the parts that might be contributing to the problem. That took another two or three weeks and more money. But now the train works.

When executives from Walt Disney World came to our laboratories and saw the train, they were blown away by the new addition since their visit just weeks before. During the ride, they were laughing and having a great time. The train and track enhanced their experience, bringing back nostalgic memories and creating an emotional connection with the Winter Wonderland concept. We continue to add new layers–like bottles of "melted snow" and machines that produce mini snow blizzards–with the goal of bringing the "Magic of Winter" alive at comfortable room temperatures.

Giving up is not an option. I will continue to research and develop Winter Wonderland until it becomes the best it can be and a reality for everyone to enjoy.

I'm here to tell you that you can fail and still, like the fabled phoenix, rise from your own ashes and fly high once again. You can do it with dogged, tenacious, determined persistence. Persistence is an entrepreneur's greatest ally; as Ralph Waldo Emerson so aptly noted, "Our greatest glory is not in never failing, but in rising up every time we fail." When it comes to entrepreneurship, the real problem isn't failure—it's learning how to deal with it and using that information to graduate to success.

An entrepreneur must learn that a setback need not be permanent. The entrepreneur who lacks the capacity to bounce back and move beyond difficulties is doomed never to taste success. It is important to learn from failure but not to wallow in it. Failure should act as a stimulus, not a paralysis.

You need to be humbled by your mistakes, not crippled by them. Pride truly goes before the fall, and entrepreneurs must always be conscious of keeping their egos in check.

From failure, you better appreciate success—how precious it is and how difficult it is to maintain. In my office, I have what I call my "Wall of Fame and Wall of Shame," made up by newspaper articles, photos of visitors, plaques and awards. It's there to remind me that the higher you go, the farther you can fall; it helps me celebrate my success but also keeps me mindful of my failures.

I would be less than honest if I told you I never had doubts about becoming a successful entrepreneur. I endured failures that made me wonder whether I'd ever make it. There was the time when my JukeBox Saturday Night club in Minneapolis was failing and my friends were abandoning me in droves. Then there were the years I couldn't find an investor for the Rainforest Cafe concept and I didn't have enough money to pay the gas bill. There were even the moments when people said I was crazy to pursue my dreams and I'd look in the mirror and wonder whether they were right. These were bad times, really bad times. I was physically and psychologically decimated. I was financially crushed. I would laugh and tell myself they were right, but I kept on going.

I persisted and prevailed, turned the corner, and walked down a new street. It wasn't easy street, but it was paved with promise and headed in the direction I wanted to go. Good things happened; success grew out of failure; the phoenix flew. But the Wall of Fame and the Wall of Shame are always there to remind me of the thin line between joy and despair, prosperity and poverty, triumph and defeat. It keeps me in the proper balance between hubris and humility, self-aggrandizement and self-deprecation. It teaches me that failure is a place I don't want to be, underscores how easy it is to make a return visit, and reminds me that perseverance is the bedrock upon which success is built.

Thomas Edison once said, “I have not failed. I’ve just found 10,000 ways that won’t work.” I love that quote, but there’s another of Edison’s that I embrace even more: “Many of life’s failures are people who did not realize how close they were to success when they gave up.”

Everyone fails, however you choose to define that. It’s how you react that can make all the difference in the ultimate outcome.

CHAPTER 19

Be Upbeat or Be Beat Down

Who cares if my glass is half empty or half full;
I still have something left to drink.

—Anonymous

Self-Examination Question:

Can you remain optimistic even when things are not going your way?

I have a motto: "I've never had a bad day."

The first time my motto got quoted in the press was on the weekend the utility workers dug a twenty-five-foot hole in the street to cut off the gas to my house. A reporter came up to me and asked how I felt. Well, I wasn't feeling exactly jovial, but I was alive and the Earth was still circling the sun. "This is a setback," I admitted. "I need to get the gas back on."

"This has got to be the worst day of your life," the reporter surmised, obviously fishing for some juicy emotional response that would read well in the morning news.

"I've never had a bad day in my life," I responded flatly. And I meant it.

I guess that's always been my philosophy: learn to deal with adversity and move on. I consider myself to be lucky. Sure, I've had some rough times; I've been hit hard and been down, but at least I've been able to pick myself up. I can put up with the gas company and a lot worse. And you can, too!

If you want to be an entrepreneur, you have to maintain an upbeat attitude in the face of disappointment and loss. You need to keep the proper perspective. When things get difficult, guess what? It comes with the territory. You're fortunate to be an entrepreneur. You get to do your own thing and be your own boss. If it comes with certain costs, like suffering through some rough times, try to think like I do: proclaim there have been cloudy days, rainy days, tornado and hurricane days . . . *but never a bad day.*

Believe me—there have been some days that have tried my patience and tempted me to renounce my motto. One of those days involved a showing of my Rainforest Cafe concept. An important investor was scheduled to take the tour, and I had rented a baboon to greet him at the front door and walk him inside. The baboon was dressed up and in the car on the way to my house when, about a mile away, it ripped its clothes off and smeared its excrement all over everything.

I learned that day it is a Guinness-level feat to sanitize a baboon covered in excrement, dress it, and bring its body odor to an acceptable level—all in ten minutes while working out of a gas station restroom in the dead of winter. The baboon went on with the show, but after that experience, we always had an ample supply of baboon diapers on hand. Just to be on the safe side.

Then there was Easter Sunday 1995. At three o'clock in the morning, I got a call from security at the Mall of America informing me that our main three-thousand-gallon fish tank at Rainforest Cafe had exploded. (Thank the Lord it hadn't happened at three o'clock in the afternoon when the restaurant was open. Who knows how many injuries would have occurred?) We had a few short hours to clean up the monumental mess, but we got it done and were open for business on schedule at 11 a.m. . . . with no one realizing what had happened. We put a large wrapper around the broken tank with a sign saying the fish were on vacation and we were making an exhibit that was bigger and better for customers to enjoy. We turned a potential disaster into a public relations coup. What could have been viewed as a disaster was now seen as something positive, a construction project to enhance the customers' dining experience at the restaurant.

Years later, at 4 p.m. on March 17, 2014, another massive fish tank teeming with exotic fish suddenly burst, leaving a huge stream of water gushing onto tables while guests were dining. This time, it was at T-REX in Downtown Disney right at prime-time dining, where wait lines often exceed two hours.

The management and waitstaff sprang into action, directing guests to safety while grabbing every bin and trash can to hold the water spill and barricading the tank in case it exploded. T-REX team members crawled into the tank with goggles and a net, scooping up the fish to keep them alive. All the guests were taken care of, with many meals being comped by the restaurant.

Rainforest Cafe with the first double-archway walk-through aquarium at the Mall of America in Bloomington, Minnesota.

The video and photos of that day went viral. Headlines on social and news media included: "Diners at Downtown Disney's T-REX in Orlando were treated to a wet and wild dining experience when a giant fish tank sprung a leak on Monday afternoon," "A fish tank at a Disney World restaurant cracked open Monday, almost giving customers an 'under the sea' dining experience," "T-REX fish tank bursts, servers jump in to save fish," and so on. T-REX received unprecedented media coverage by FOX News, Huffington Post, Travelers Today, and the *Orlando Sentinel*, to name a few.

The handling of this disaster by management and employees turned an unfortunate situation into great public relations for T-REX, and the staff was praised for their swift and professional response. Most importantly all the fish were saved.

I also recall moments when my financial resources were running on empty. One time I was walking to a meeting with my accountant and close friend, Tim Myslajek. Along the way, there was a restaurant with an ornate wishing well situated near the front door. I stopped to dig out some coins from my pocket and make a wish. I couldn't find a single penny to toss into the well. That's how broke I was. I was totally out of money. Tim looked at me sadly and said, "This is a *really* bad day for you."

And I replied, "There's no such thing as a bad day."

Sometimes, maintaining an upbeat attitude can be even more challenging than just being short on cash. Sadly, I got a phone call

Diners at Downtown Disney's T-REX in Orlando were treated to a wet and wild dining experience when a giant fish tank sprung a leak." On March 17, 2014, T-REX servers jumped in the tanks and saved all the fish.

from a friend of mine whom I had been trying to reach. He apologized for being out of touch but explained that his mother was diagnosed with cancer and told she had only a few days left.

She was ninety-three years old. The priest who administered last rites asked her to what she owed her longevity.

"Two things," she replied without missing a beat, "exercise and vodka."

That showed remarkable dignity and optimism, being able to keep her sense of humor right up to the very end. She was faced with a moment in life that most people would be terrified to get to, and yet she did not let that affect her personality and attitude. She enjoyed every aspect of life and made sure those around her were enjoying it too. She will be remembered with respect and admiration for being able to look on the brighter side of things. Right up to the very end.

You have a choice: be upbeat or be beat down. And remember that the best way never to have a bad day (at least where business and finances are concerned) is to convince yourself you won't.

Walt Disney once said, "All our dreams can come true—if we have the courage to pursue them." So have faith in yourself. Be a person of courage. Stand erect and move forward into the storm; the winds will subside and the sun will shine. Keep your eye on your dream and stay a steady course. Let your persistence, your bulldog determination, see you through to your goal. As you move forward, be guided by the words of Winston Churchill: "Never, never, never, never give up."

SECTION IV

PEOPLE

CHAPTER 20

Have a Caring Attitude Toward All Living Things

I will pay more for the ability to deal with people than any other ability under the sun.

—John D. Rockefeller

Self-Examination Question:

Do you care about the feelings and needs of others and do what you can to help them achieve their personal goals?

Think back for a moment and identify someone you really respect—somebody for whom, if asked to go to the ends of the Earth, you would make the trip. Chances are this somebody is a person who shares those same feelings about you.

When it comes to making friends, influencing people, and being a good parent, spouse, or business partner, one of the most critical things you can do is genuinely care for those around you. People respond positively when they believe you care about them; they want to be around you, to be your friend, to do business with you. A willingness to care for others—and to *show* that caring attitude—is so important when building relationships. I still carry around a quote from a book I read a long time ago. It says, simply, "If you care, you are there."

I am not speaking of tolerating someone or pretending to care about someone so you can get something from him or her. A mercenary individual might be able to bluff for a while, but, in any meaningful long-term relationship, such manipulative, insincere behavior will be discovered—and the consequences won't be pretty. Caring is something that should flow honestly from the heart, from a true sense of concern for others, not from the head, where one puts forth a robotic, intellectual effort to feign caring in search of personal gain. It is the ability to react quickly when someone needs help. When I was driving to work a number of years ago, I saw a woman driving erratically. She was in a ditch, and her car kept hitting the guardrail. I sped up my car to see what was going on and noticed that her head was bobbing back and forth. She was obviously having a seizure.

I passed her and pulled over to the side of the road. I ran across three lanes of traffic and managed to catch up to the car (which was still moving). The door was locked with the woman trapped inside. I pulled off one of my shoes, put it over my fist, smashed the window, and jumped in to stop the car. The public service department gave me an award for saving her life, but the greatest award was being lucky enough to be there to help her.

I know of a very successful businessman who has a sign on his office desk that reads, "What you think of me is none of my business." For some, that is their preferred business outlook. They focus on the trade, not the trader; the business deal, not the person making it.

I don't feel this way at all. What you think of me is very much my business. In fact, my business depends on it. That's because I can't effectively do business with people who don't care about me, and, conversely, I can build a much more effective business relationship with people who do.

As an example, I remember when officials from Kansas City first approached me about putting our first T-REX restaurant in their town. A gentleman named Steve Graham called me multiple times trying to get a conversation started about the project. I remember telling him that Kansas City wasn't "on our map"—meaning a high-density tourist location, which we previously identified by putting pins on a map in our office.

He continued to call, and I kept repeating the "map" response.

"I'm bringing a pin with me so that I can stick it in Kansas City on your map," Steve announced. "Then it will be there!"

I not only had to laugh but also admired his persistence. He introduced me to Dan Lowe, who was his boss at the time, and the city council. He then introduced me to the mayor of Kansas City, who, as it happened, was a former schoolteacher. She was enthused beyond her wildest dreams about the prospect of having a concept that could be both interactive and educational. She became a significant player, ultimately asking me what it would take to bring T-REX to Kansas City. I responded quite frankly that it would take 100 percent commitment to raise the funds, including my request that we not have to pay any money back. I wanted the money to be a gift toward promoting the restaurant as a magnet to attract other restaurateurs, retail stores, and entertainment.

No one thought there was even a chance that would happen. Lo and behold, the city got together, and it raised the funds, and we did not have to pay the money back. Everyone was in shock.

Initially, I wasn't very excited at the overall project. But when I met with the contingent from Kansas City and saw how much they cared about me and T-REX, it made a real difference. Instead of being talked into a deal, I *wanted* to work with them and make a deal, which is exactly what happened.

If I sense that a customer or investor doesn't seem to care about me, it disturbs me, and I want to know why. I'll ask questions or do what's necessary to discover where the problem lies. I want to correct the behavior that is causing the problem—not because I want the person's business (although I might) but because I care about people and I am unhappy if someone is disturbed by something I'm doing.

Now, you can't satisfy everybody, and, because of basic human nature, there will always be some people who don't think highly of you, no matter how much you care for them. If you cannot find a reasonable explanation for their behavior, chalk it up to chemistry or some other esoteric factor that makes certain people incompatible, and then move on. There will always be more people who will be happy to work with you than those who won't.

CHAPTER 21

Make People Feel Special

Pretend that every single person you meet has a sign around his or her neck that says, 'Make Me Feel Important.' Not only will you succeed in sales, you will succeed in life.

—Mary Kay Ash

Self-Examination Question:

When was the last time you did something just to make somebody feel special?

Think about times in your life you've been singled out by somebody who made you feel special. Maybe this person praised you, or gave you an unexpected gift, or took the time to write a letter on your behalf. How did you feel toward this person? You may use a whole range of adjectives, and I suspect all of them would be positive. People want to feel special and recognized; it's a normal human desire, and I have yet to meet an individual who doesn't appreciate this kind of attention.

I know some entrepreneurs who practice this principle at the most rudimentary level. They send out a yearly birthday card to venture capitalists and other individuals they see as relevant to their business success. They might also send out holiday greeting cards and/or congratulatory notes for significant events such as anniversaries. In a sense, the person receiving this card might feel special; on the other hand, because these events occur on a regular, annual basis, the impact value of these cards is limited. People realize that a computer can be programmed to automatically send out cards on a specific date each year, so the act doesn't take much thought or planning.

A more meaningful way to make people feel special is to recognize them or their loved ones for events that *don't* occur on a predictable, regular basis. For example, a graduation, a birth in the family, a marriage, a promotion, the receipt of an award, or membership in a special organization are all good opportunities to show you've paid attention to what is happening in their lives. Taking the time to recognize these occasions and contacting them is what will really make someone feel valued.

Another great way to make people feel special is to phone them and say hello or send a written greeting when *no* special reason is involved. The call or the card is a potent reminder that you're thinking of them, that you care about them, that they're someone special.

I appreciate others who do the same. There's a talented local attorney named David Valentini who's been very prominent in well-publicized court cases—a very busy guy. Once, I came home tired after a very long day. I checked my phone, and there was a message from David saying he just wanted to tell me how much he appreciated our friendship and how much he missed hearing from me. There was no other reason for the call.

"Love you," he said as he ended the call. "Hope you're having a great day."

I make it a point to combine all these approaches in dealing with my friends and business associates. I send out cards, and I make calls, sometimes on significant dates and sometimes on random days of my choosing.

People also feel special when you treat them as unique individuals. You can show this by taking notice of their personal lives and interests. For example, before I meet with clients or potential investors, I learn as much as I can about them. Are they married? Single? What about kids? Do they have special hobbies? Pets? I want to get to know them on a personal basis, and my interest is genuine. I think it's essential when you meet with people to be able to know the names of those who are most important in their lives.

Back in the days of our JukeBox Saturday Night club and restaurant, when we were planning to open a venue in a new city, I would first move there for a month. I wanted to meet face-to-face with the mayor, the chamber of commerce, and other important people in the community. I wanted them to feel special and know we saw their community as unique. In fact, once we opened JukeBox Saturday Night, I made it the duty of the club manager to read the town's papers to find out about all the local news. Even putting a "Congratulations Graduating Seniors" message on our sign out front was important; it showed that we were involved in the community.

Knowing more about the people you are in business with not only provides information you can use to make them feel special but also gives you insight on how to interact with them more successfully.

A case in point: when we were pitching T-REX to officials in Kansas City, I needed to meet with the mayor to get her approval. When I found out she had been a schoolteacher, I decided to focus my restaurant presentation on an interest the mayor shared: the interactive, educational aspects of the venture. I shared with her how child focus groups helped us to develop a simulated fossil dig; and dinosaur information kits as an interactive learning experience. The mayor appreciated this aspect of our restaurant and gave the project a glowing review when she reported back to her political associates in Kansas City. She was a big part of the reason we got a generous financial grant to open T-REX in the city.

Knowing enough about your client, customer, or investor to discover points of common interest can really make the individual feel special (everyone enjoys the chance to talk with someone about what he or she likes and thus more likely to support the project or idea you're recommending).

When a friend or associate is having trouble, I'll pick up the phone and give that person a call to provide reassurance and let him or her know there are friends out there who care. Sometimes the person I call will want to vent. I listen. Sometimes he or she asks for advice. I'll give it if I think I'm qualified to respond.

J. C. Penney said, "Every business is built on friendship."

Sometimes, great friendships can begin under the most unusual circumstances. In 2016, I went to get a complete physical at the Mayo Clinic in Rochester, Minnesota. One of the things scheduled was a colonoscopy.

I undressed—including socks and underwear—and put on a robe they had given me. Then, I went to a waiting room—along with several other semi-nude men—to wait my turn for the procedure. I sat down across from a gentleman who had his eyeglasses on, reading an iPad. Next to him stood a gentleman who was fully clothed. (This seemed odd, since he was the only man in the room who was completely dressed.)

It took me two minutes to become completely bored. *Jeopardy!* was on the television, and I asked the man across from me if he minded if I put on the news.

The gentleman took his glasses off and gave me the biggest smile that I have ever seen in my life: "Sir, I don't mind at all."

We introduced ourselves. His name was Fouad Mashal, and he was from Abu Dhabi. I told him I was in the restaurant business.

"What a small world," he replied. "I feed 150,000 people a day in Abu Dhabi."

Surprised, I asked how that was possible, and he explained that he built and owned many apartments, restaurants, hospitals, and other facilities. As part of the employment contract, he provided three meals a day. I immediately suggested that we should be doing something together and invited him to visit my laboratories in Minneapolis.

The next thing I knew, a doctor walked in the room and told Fouad that they were ready to perform his procedure. I asked the doctor to wait (what a switch—a patient keeping an M.D. waiting!) while we made plans to meet after we were done with our procedures, so we could continue our conversation.

After the two-hour procedure, groggy and still under anesthesia, I woke and immediately asked the nurses where my friend was. Unbeknownst to me, Fouad was also waking up and groggy at roughly the same time asking where his friend Steve was!

When we both got out to the lobby, we exchanged stories about looking for one another and enjoyed a great laugh. We then went to a local restaurant and had a two-hour conversation over a great meal.

Fouad and his executive and security guard, Hourani Wissam, were planning to fly to Las Vegas for business, but I convinced them to cancel their trip and visit my laboratories in Minneapolis instead. I also invited them to come to Orlando and visit the restaurants I created. That's exactly what they decided to do. They canceled all their appointments and called one of Fouad's sons—who was in Montreal—to have him fly in and meet us. They went through my laboratories in Minnesota, flew to Orlando, went to all of our restaurants in Disney, and then the following day flew to Chicago and met my partners, the Gibsons Restaurant Group.

An incredible friendship started at the Mayo Clinic in Rochester while preparing to get a colonoscopy. Later, my wife Sunhi and I received an invitation to Abu Dhabi. Fouad hosted us in luxury and treated us like royalty with first-class tickets and accommodations at the Emirates Palace hotel that the sheikh had built for himself. It truly felt like we were part of the family. We saw the most amazing sights and came to admire their country and culture. The business empire that Fouad built is impressive. We are looking forward to not only doing business together but also, more importantly, being lifelong friends.

It's like Fouad and I are brothers from another mother. He is Muslim. I am Jew. If only the rest of the world could see how easily a relationship could be formed when you put effort into caring about another person.

It's valuable to remember that making people feel special can involve relatively small things. Management professor and author Dr. Michael LeBoeuf sums it up this way: "There are two things people want more than sex and money . . . recognition and praise." Let your team members know you appreciate their time, effort, and accomplishments. Public praise goes a long way. I am blessed with a tremendous team of dedicated men and women who are a large part of the company's success. My hard-working staff deserves recognition, and so does yours.

CHAPTER 22

Help Others Achieve Their Goals

Successful people are always looking for opportunities to help others. Unsuccessful people are always asking, 'What's in it for me?'

—Brian Tracy

Self-Examination Question:

Are you willing to help other people succeed whenever possible?

In my entrepreneurial career, I have gained great benefits—in terms of both personal satisfaction and professional advancement—by helping other people reach their goals and objectives. You don't have to believe in karma to follow this recommendation, but, if what comes around truly does go around, then my suggestion certainly can't hurt.

There's something euphoric about helping people, sharing your knowledge and perspective with those who seek you out for advice.

Many people will call me for business advice or even when they're having trouble getting a table at one of my restaurants. No matter if I am juggling seven other things, I will always take the call. It is a great feeling being able to confirm reservations knowing they will be taken care of. It is also beneficial for me because I can stay in touch with the on-site management at my establishments.

While driving one day, I noticed a car parked on the side of the road with a flat tire. A gentleman in a suit was digging through his trunk, presumably looking to change the tire, and he did not look like he would enjoy walking a couple of miles to get to a car repair garage. So I gave him a lift to a gas station.

In conversation, we learned that we had a good friend in common, an executive of a huge company. Talk about a small world. Later, I heard that he posted our meeting on the Internet with the hope that it would encourage others to look for opportunities to help those in need.

Many years ago, a woman attended a workshop where I had given a speech on the joys of being an entrepreneur. At the time, she had been thinking of buying a business; after my presentation, she decided to go the entrepreneurial route and develop a business of her own. Her name is Maxine Clark, and (as you might remember from Chapter 14) she founded Build-A-Bear, a fantastically successful plush toy empire. Years later, it was Maxine whom I approached to form a strategic partnership. Our Build-A-Dino product line at T-REX brought in more revenue for her company by complementing her existing products. It brought a demographic she had been missing out on, young boys, into her store. Was our partnership a coincidence? Certainly. As I had unknowingly helped Maxine toward her goal of starting a new business, Build-A-Bear, she turned around and helped me achieve mine. Build-A-Dino is now one of our top revenue generators in retail.

Maribeth Bisienere, the senior vice president for Walt Disney World Parks, had asked me to give a speech on leadership to some of the Disney team members. I couldn't be there on the date she needed, so I made a video and sent it to her. About a year later, I was with her on a business trip to visit Disney's Paris operation. During the trip, she met with a French businessman, the owner of a tethered balloon company, regarding a joint venture. We got engaged in a conversation where we came up with new ideas for his business.

Later, Maribeth shared that the time I took to make the video and to help her French business associate made a big impact on her. She told me, "Because of your willingness to share and help others, I'm much more apt to do business with you." Now I have T-REX, Yak & Yeti, and the Boathouse at Disney. A friend of mine always says, "No good deed goes unrewarded." I must agree with her.

Being a successful entrepreneur comes with responsibilities that go beyond the fiduciary duties of everyday business. You have a responsibility to help others achieve their goals just as you achieved yours, because you have more opportunities and resources than others to give back.

While reading the Minnesota Business Journal, a thought occurred to me: I would love to learn and read about local entrepreneurs and what made them successful. I approached the Journal and offered to write a monthly column free of charge where I would interview entrepreneurs and share their secrets and motivations for success. The editors loved the idea, and we were able to write that column for four years. It was fun seeking out entrepreneurs who were just starting out, as well as some of the big names, including

Bill Murray: actor, comedian, and part owner of the Saint Paul Saints baseball team. It took a lot of phone calls to get ahold of Bill, but, lo and behold, I got through to him and had a two-hour conversation over the phone.

The story was a huge hit, becoming the front cover piece for that month. It set the tone for us getting three other cover stories published. There is a list of fifty people we have written articles about who received positive visibility and notoriety. How cool is it to be in the spotlight and then be able to shine that light on someone else?

Out of writing these articles came the idea of writing and publishing *It's a Jungle in There.*

While trying to find a publisher for the first edition of the book, I turned to Harvey Mackay, the best-selling author (and Minneapolis celebrity) who appeared back in Chapter 14. I had learned a lot from Harvey, watching how he responded to people's needs for his time or advice, and I wanted to see whether he thought I was headed in the right direction.

In the middle of running his envelope company, writing a new book, and speaking all over the world, Harvey took me from grade school level to a master's degree in book publishing—promoting and marketing, how to successfully get TV and radio interviews, and what companies to hire. He gave a remarkable amount of time and energy to help me, and I'll never forget it.

When I first spoke with the venture capitalist Lyle Berman, it was to pitch him on the idea for Rainforest Cafe. Over the course of two and a half years, I learned as much as I could about Grand Casino, which Lyle had created in Hinckley, Minnesota. He wanted to open a couple of restaurants, and I offered him help in that area of business. Lyle opened two award-winning restaurants, one called the Carousel Bar and another called the Grand American Barbecue, which later became Famous Dave's. Sure enough, Lyle became my angel investor in Rainforest Cafe, and Famous Dave Anderson wrote the first check.

If I hadn't tried to help Lyle achieve his goals, he would not have become my angel investor. Because I first helped him, Lyle made my dream of Rainforest Cafe a reality.

Steven and friends celebrate the eighty-fifth birthday of Lee Iacocca (fifth from right) in Las Vegas, Nevada. John Goodman (third from left) and Nasser Kazeminy (fourth from left) helped fund the research and development for T-REX.

CHAPTER 23

Managing Perception for Maximum Impact

All the world's a stage;
how do you wish to be seen by your audience?

—English author, unknown

Self-Examination Question:

Do you change your behavior to influence a person's perception of you?

I've written a word just below this sentence. Take a moment, if you would, and read the word aloud:

Unionized.

What did you think of? If you are like most people, you read the word in a way that describes a business organization where workers are represented by a union. One would say the company is "unionized." That is because the majority of us spend most of our time working with people and dealing with organizations where unions are part of the business landscape. However, what if you were a biochemist? Then you might read the word in a different way: *un-ionized.* Why? Because ions are more common than labor unions in your line of work and your frame of reference, and we know people perceive the world differently based on their experiences and beliefs.

In the world of interpersonal relationships, you can use what social scientists refer to as "perception management" to influence the way people perceive you. Perception management involves acting in certain ways to create in others a specific impression of you—hopefully a positive impression. If you use it effectively, you can head off a lot of serious problems and interpersonal conflicts.

For example, when we first opened our Rainforest Cafe, PETA decided to protest the restaurant's use of live parrots. Organization members were quite vocal about their feelings and even threw what appeared to be blood at some of our restaurant staff. We were angry and hurt. No one loves animals and birds more than I do, particularly parrots; I've had them as pets since I was a teenager. The question was, what should we do about the protests?

We decided to use perception management. Several of us joined PETA, and, the next time the protesters gathered in front of the restaurant, we went outside, showed them our PETA membership cards, and indicated we were one of them. We explained to the protesters that our birds were not taken from the wild. They were hand-raised, domestically fed babies. We loved our birds—and what was wrong with that?

The PETA protesters went away.

Another time, I faced a different kind of crisis. We had decided to hold a major fundraiser for some political candidates at my Jukebox Saturday Night club and restaurant. At that time, there was an up-and-coming union involved in organizing restaurants and hotels in Minnesota. The organization decided to make a statement by trying to unionize my team. The union knew that politicians normally respect picket lines, so union members decided to throw pickets around my place and stop the political candidates from entering my establishment. They actually had a guy dressed in a huge, furry rat costume standing near our front door with a picket sign in his hand. He was probably the only comfortable person on the picket line; it was a windy winter evening in the bitterly cold Twin Cities.

I decided to try a little perception management. The people on that picket line had a very negative opinion of us, so I asked my team to make some hot cocoa and chocolate chip cookies and bring them out to the protesters, who drank the cocoa, ate the cookies . . . and left! What was supposed to be a five-hour protest lasted fifteen minutes. Our goodwill helped alter the picketers' perception of us as "bad guys" and helped create a behavioral outcome that we dearly wanted. It also got us good press; observers were so impressed by our gesture and how it defused the situation that it was in the paper the next day.

Perception management can be very effective in creating the appropriate image or belief you want people to have about you and your work. Because I wanted people to see JukeBox Saturday Night as a wholesome, clean, fun place to party, rather than a tough joint with hard drinking and barroom brawls, I used perception management to underscore this atmosphere. We used words to create the appropriate environment. For example, we didn't have "bouncers"; we employed "doormen." Bouncers are big, muscular, and intimidating, while our doormen were neatly dressed and welcomed guests to the club in a friendly, conversational manner. I also employed a "master of ceremonies" instead of a "disc jockey." Our master of ceremonies did more than spin records. He knew how to communicate with people of all ages and backgrounds.

Perception management is about getting people to see you and what you do in a positive light. I learned the importance of perception management as a teenager, back when I was running the poker game at the Silver Gull Beach Club. There I was, pocketing hundreds of dollars a weekend with no problems until I started bragging about my good fortune. By opening my big mouth, I shot myself in the foot. People get jealous, and jealous people will do their best to bring down the object of their jealousy. If I had remained silent and just gone about my business, I might have kept my summer windfall going for another five years. As it was, my bragging cost me a dream job.

Shooting off my mouth was a failure of perception management. It violated a cardinal rule: when you're doing well, keep quiet and don't reveal the degree of your success to others. Be particularly careful not to boast or brag about how much money you make. Never forget that jealousy is everywhere and that, when it comes to money, people are definitely concerned and jealous over how much others make. You can say all day long that people don't care about how much money a person makes, but it just isn't true. People do care, and they care enough to sabotage individuals who flaunt their riches or shove their good fortune in other people's faces.

A friend once told me, "Get rich in the dark." I never quite understood what he meant until I experienced my summer job debacle. Now I understand it fully and live by his dictum as best I can.

As a final example of perception management, let me describe a conflict that arose over the appropriate start time for our T-REX grand opening at Disney World. We had planned to have the party from 2 to 4 p.m. Then, Disney called and suggested an earlier time frame—11 a.m. to 1 p.m.—to make it easier for reporters to get coverage ready for the evening news. We thought about it a long time and decided that an eleven o'clock opening was not celebratory or special; it was lunch hour. The later time slot made the ribbon-cutting ceremony something special. It came down to the difference between perceiving the opening ceremony as "lunch" or a "reception," and we opted for the latter.

Image is important when you're trying to create the appropriate mind-set. Perception management is a way you, as an entrepreneur, can shape your image to fit the way you want to be perceived by others.

CHAPTER 24

Create Positive Press

Smiling faces make you happy,
and good news makes you feel better.

—Proverbs 15:30

Self-Examination Question:

Do you make a concerted effort to establish good media contacts and have them generate positive publicity for the work that you do?

Some entrepreneurs seem to have a love-hate relationship with the press. This is unfortunate. Getting media attention—*positive* attention—is critical for a large number of entrepreneurs. In fact, publicity might be the lifeblood of their creations. Without it, the creations die.

I actively seek media attention in my business operations. In fact, when dealing with reporters and other members of the media, I have a "two-hour" rule: I personally return all media calls within two hours of the time I receive them. I've learned to respect other people's time, and I know that many reporters are working against deadlines. It's not only common courtesy that makes me follow my two-hour rule but also the realization that the faster I call back, the better the chance a story about my work will be written or aired or that my involvement in a particular story will be included.

I also answer my own phone. Members of the media are often shocked by this, since they expect to run a gauntlet of gatekeepers before reaching me. I've found that they appreciate this personal touch—a sentiment often reflected in their willingness to give me more time and coverage in their stories. When speaking with the media, I try to give reporters and newscasters everything they ask for—and more. I'm always looking for additional angles or news I can feed them that might whet their appetites for extra information on what I'm doing. Many times, a reporter has asked me a question that was to be a small part of a story and, by the end of the conversation, my project or commentary had become the major focus of the article. As I said in an earlier chapter, you're selling not only your product but also yourself.

Reporters want to share quality stories, so if you can help them by providing information and, at the same time, exude enthusiasm, it's going to make a positive difference in the way you're portrayed in the media. "PR" is an abbreviation for "public relations," but it could also stand for "personal relationships." The personal relationship you establish with the media will influence the quality of public relations you receive.

Knowing the right people can also generate good press for you and your business. Don't shy away from meeting and building relationships with highly accomplished people. Networking with well-known personalities not only is critical for expanding your base of operations but also for building face recognition and generating good opportunities for publicity. Getting to know influential people can occur anytime and anywhere, such as while sitting on a cross-country flight. Take advantage of such chance encounters to build new relationships. As an active member in political fundraising, I have had the privilege of getting to know and becoming friends with several nationally elected officials.

One great way to generate good press for your product or your company is often overlooked by otherwise savvy entrepreneurs: your telephone answering system. I have always believed that your first contact with a potential customer, investor, or client is critically important, and that first contact is often by phone. Therefore, what the caller hears when your phone is answered is crucial and can go a long way to encourage or discourage further interest in you or what you have to offer.

If you can afford it, I think it is wise to invest in a human operator so that the first thing a caller hears when dialing up your business is a real person, *not* a machine. Moreover, whether your phone system employs a person or a machine, it is important that the call be answered in a timely fashion. Waiting more than five rings to hear a response turns a caller off. Further, a caller should not be placed on hold for more than a minute. (If hold times are longer than a minute, one way to reduce the chance of losing callers is to provide a "countdown system" where the caller is informed how long the expected wait time will be. It is important that the wait time experienced does not exceed the wait time promised.)

That hold time provides an opportunity that is often overlooked: the chance to give a captive audience a great sales pitch. Canned music or dead silence during wait times is ridiculous. Give yourself some good press right there on the telephone. Maybe you can even sell the caller before you ever pick up the phone!

Websites are another great tool to generate positive press. A good website favorably reflects you and your company's ideas, products, and/or services. It needs to be easily navigated and provide visitors with obvious ways to contact you and/or your company. An attractive, well-organized, useful website is one of the great advertising tools in the entrepreneur's arsenal. Reporters and other members of the media will often decide whether to interview you based on the impressions they get from your website. Make those impressions positive and impactful.

Since writing the first edition of this book, social media outlets have exploded. Because these formats are so instantaneous, it's important that you're more careful than ever about what you say, how you say it, and your delivery method. Most companies today have somebody who specializes in their social media campaigns. We have such a person at the Boathouse. Unlike printed press or radio and television, which have sporadic schedules, social media is something that we can utilize every day. It's consistent, it's constant, and it's evolutionary. Handling social media the right way will give you the best and fastest results in terms of positive press.

Here is one fun suggestion for generating good press: throw a party! Perhaps this is a predictable recommendation coming from a themed restaurant owner. But doing a good job of hosting people at a social function is a great way to get positive exposure and press. When I throw a party, I want it to be special because that is the message I want to send to my guests: *you are special*. I ban "blah" birthday cakes at birthday parties—you know, the frosted layer cake or the sheet cake, your standard kind of dessert. What I want to give my guests is something different—like ice cream that arrives in a classic Good Humor ice cream truck, reminiscent of the good old days, served up by the Good Humor man dressed in all white. And it's important to remember the details. If I'm serving finger foods, I want to make sure there are ample napkins and toothpicks in easy reach and beverages that have plenty of clean glasses and ice. There should also be enough trash cans so guests do not need to go hunting for them and enough catering staff to best assist the guests.

If you're lucky enough to be invited to a party, go. Even if you don't feel like it—if you're an introvert or you have a heavy appointment schedule—try to make time to drop by. You don't have to stay long. By showing up, your presence validates the effort your host went through to plan the event and strengthens your relationship. Plus, there's always the chance for a little networking with other guests.

CHAPTER 25

The Power of Trust in Transactions

If people like you, they'll listen to you,
but if they trust you, they'll do business with you.

—Zig Ziglar

Self-Examination Question:

Do you recognize the crucial role trust plays in successful business?

Trust is the bedrock upon which all meaningful human relationships are built, and I've learned that, in my business, an entrepreneur is no better than his or her word. Trust is critical to potential investors because they're buying you as well as what you have to offer. If they can't trust you, how can they invest in you?

William Shakespeare wrote, "No legacy is so rich as honesty."

Trust is the foundation for all meaningful relationships with honesty as the base. If you have conducted your affairs in an honest manner, you will always be able to look your investors in the eye (and yourself in the mirror), even if the venture fails. People will risk taking a second chance because they trust what you say. In the 1990s, I was invited to appear before a group of Disney executives to discuss the possibility of placing a Rainforest Cafe in one of the company's theme parks. Disney, obviously, is very concerned about its image, and that includes the people with whom the company does business. The term "squeaky-clean" comes to mind when trying to describe what Disney is looking for when it screens team members, vendors, and business partners.

On the day of my presentation, I was ushered into a large boardroom where several Disney executives were sitting around a conference table. Before I even had a chance to present my prepared statement, one of the executives asked me a question: "How do you think Disney feels about gambling? Isn't Lyle Berman, chairman of your board [of Rainforest Cafe], involved in gaming?"

"Yes, he is," I answered. "And he does a great job and gives hundreds of Native Americans jobs."

The executive, Mr. Bud Dare, considered my answer for a moment, looked at me intently, and offered up another question: "I understand you had a place called JukeBox Saturday Night, and, for a while, you had topless dancing on the second floor. How do you think Disney feels about that?"

I remember thinking to myself at that point that Disney was a dead deal. I felt like I had just been kicked in the groin. Between Lyle's involvement with gaming and the issues of topless dancing at my nightclub, what chance did I have to get Disney on board with my project? I could feel myself begin to sweat profusely. I did the only thing I knew how to do: I answered his question with complete candor and honesty.

I fully disclosed what had happened at JukeBox Saturday Night. I explained how we had suffered a financial setback and owed money in taxes. I described how our nightclub and restaurant weren't doing well and how somebody had come to us and asked to rent out the second floor of our building for limited adult entertainment. I admitted I never should have done it, that I regretted my decision. I explained that we shut the operation down as quickly as we could. The people had a one-week lease, and, when it was up, we didn't renew it. I took responsibility for my mistake, acknowledging that the problem had occurred on my watch, and shouldered the full blame for it.

After answering the difficult questions, I began my formal presentation. I did the best I could under the circumstances but was worried it wouldn't be enough.

When I finally heard the news that Disney had given us the green light to go ahead with the restaurant plans, I was both pleased and surprised.

A few years later, I had a chance to speak again with Mr. Dare about Disney's decision and what had happened that day back in the conference room. I learned that the Disney executives knew everything about me ahead of time, including the adult entertainment snafu at JukeBox Saturday Night. If I hadn't been totally honest with them and expressed my remorse over what had happened at my club, the executive told me candidly, the deal probably would have never gone through.

When I first acquired the barn that ultimately became Green Acres Event Center, its zoning was very limited. My initial intent was to use the place for storage, but, after many suggestions from the community, it occurred to me that it could be so much more. So I began working on the necessary changes, renovations, and other jobs.

In my enthusiasm, I did not first obtain the necessary permits. The cute white picket fence around the barn's perimeter added to its charm and helped keep the inspectors, licensing people, and zoning officials at arm's length.

It worked until it didn't. One day I left the front gate open, and a city inspector walked up and asked what I was doing. Instead of trying to bluster my way around him, I shared with him all of the improvements, which were being done without the permits, and told him the truth of what I was up to.

Because I was so forthright, we developed an instant friendship, and, instead of red tagging the project, he came every weekend with his own set of tools and helped me with the work. But he also made certain that I filled out the proper legal forms and applied for the needed permits. He became an ally and helped me meet government regulations.

The city of Eden Prairie, surprisingly for its size, did not have an event center. Due to so many requests from the community to use the barn for weddings, birthday parties, and other activities, I approached a member of the city council, Ron Case (he's running for mayor as I write this). I shared with him and his wife Kathie the letters of support I had received regarding the barn. I explained how the idea would benefit the community–and I admitted to not going through the legal process for the work I had completed to date. They appreciated my honesty and became the biggest supporters for the venue. Ron and Kathie Case were instrumental in Green Acres becoming the first event center in Eden Prairie.

With the Cases's aid and guidance, the city council voted 7-0 in favor of everything that I needed, from zoning changes to building permits to licensing, even the ability to offer horse-drawn hayrides through the city parks. Through the power of developing a mutually respectful and trusting relationship, Green Acres Event Center is now a thriving venue and integral part of the Eden Prairie community.

CHAPTER 26

Don't Burn Bridges (Just Cross Them Carefully the Second Time Around)

Never cut what you can untie.

—Joseph Joubert

Self-Examination Question:

Are you willing to give a person many second chances?

At some point in your entrepreneurial life (maybe at many points), somebody is going to disappoint you or take advantage of you. When this happens, should you just write the person off and decide never to work with him or her again? There's a real temptation to say yes and be done with this type of individual for good. Why not? The person has either let you down or screwed you up.

But wait a moment. People change. Times change. Conditions change. Individuals who hurt you in the past might be able to help you in the future, so I wouldn't be so quick to dismiss them out of hand. I'd just be a lot more cautious in dealing with them the second time around.

Some of my biggest opportunities and successful ventures have involved people who, earlier in my life, caused me disappointment. Take, for example, my own father, Jules. He left home when I was young, pretty much abandoning our family, and, for a long time, we were estranged. Yet he is the person responsible for getting me together with Lyle Berman, the venture capitalist who would eventually become my angel investor, providing the resources needed to make my Rainforest Cafe dream a reality.

How did my dad do it? With a lot of nerve and chutzpah.

He was working in Las Vegas at the time and had gone to watch the World Series of Poker. While he was there, he noticed that one of the players was Lyle, whom he recognized as a venture capitalist from Minnesota. When play was halted for a fifteen-minute bathroom break, my father actually snuck by security and sat down in Lyle's chair, right in front of $350,000 in chips. When Lyle returned, he was in for a shock: my father was sitting in his chair as if he was ready to play the next hand of poker. Once he got over his initial surprise, Lyle asked my dad to get up and leave.

"Sir," said my dad, looking Lyle in the eye, "I'm not going until you agree to meet my son who lives in Minneapolis."

At that point, Lyle started to call for a security guard to throw my dad out. But he stopped when my dad pulled a fifty-dollar bill from his pocket and said, "Here, this is for you. You've *got* to meet my son. He's got a great concept for a restaurant you have to see to believe."

Steven thanks his father, Jules Schussler, with a bronze sculpture of Walt Disney and Mickey Mouse at the 1996 opening ceremonies of Rainforest Cafe at Downtown Disney in Orlando, Florida. By pitching the Rainforest Cafe concept to Lyle Berman, Jules connected Steven to the investor who would help fuel one of the most successful themed restaurant chains in the country.

At that point, Lyle realized where my dad was coming from. He was accustomed to people pitching him ideas, just not from his chair at the World Series of Poker. So he gave my father his fifty dollars back and handed him a business card. "Have your son call my assistant and set up an appointment," he said, "and please get out of my seat."

My dad went directly home and called me at three o'clock in the morning, described what he had done, and told me to schedule an appointment. I did as he said, and, as the TV newscasters are fond of saying, "The rest is history."

Crazy, isn't it? My dad, who had been one of my biggest disappointments in his role as a father, came through for me much later in his life. After my father left, I thought the bridge was burned between us—but it wasn't. I'm glad to say we reconciled and shared some good times together before he died a few years ago.

There have been many other times when my commitment not to burn bridges has proven beneficial. My most dramatic business example involves Landry's, the restaurant chain that purchased Rainforest Cafe at a fire-sale price. I was unhappy with the sale when it happened. I thought we could have done better and tried to raise capital to take the company private. I got together with David Siegel (the largest time-share owner in the world), Herb and Mel Simon (at the time, owners of Mall of America), and Robert Earl (owner of Planet Hollywood) to see whether a deal could be achieved, but we failed. In the end Landry's won out, and I remember expressing my frustration to the top executive at Landry's, Tilman Fertitta, who was instrumental in making the purchase. Not only did Tilman win the financial battle but also he made changes to the restaurant that were antithetical to my beliefs about what I thought the restaurant should be and what it should represent.

From my vantage point, Tilman, who is as passionate about his business as I am about my creations, had changed my vision at Rainforest Cafe. To make matters worse, he proclaimed that the acquisition of Rainforest Cafe was one of his greatest business decisions—and was quick to mention how he had purchased the properties at such a great price. Talk about rubbing salt in the wound! And, to top it off, once he had control of Rainforest, he re-engineered the menu, including our signature, world-famous Rasta pasta dish by changing the bowtie pasta that was an integral part of the selection's appeal. I decided that Tilman Fertitta was a brash, arrogant, bargain-basement, bottom-feeding, business-acquisition nemesis.

As I was working on this most recent version of the book, I was tempted to take out the last sentence in the preceding paragraph.

Instead, I decided to leave it in and expand on it a bit more. At the time I wrote the original sentence, I was still upset about the sale of Rainforest Cafe and projected that disappointment at Tilman. Now, through objective lenses, I can see that Tilman is a smart and savvy businessman who made sound business decisions. There's nothing wrong with being a bargain-basement, bottom-feeding, business-acquisition nemesis. That's how he became one of the most successful restaurateurs in the country.

But my point is that since Tilman bought Rainforest Cafe (not to mention the Houston Rockets and many other properties), I have spent a great amount of time with him and his family, especially two of his sons, Michael and Patrick. They've visited Minnesota to see our laboratories and tour five new restaurant concepts that we've created. The passion and excitement they showed for our new creations is heartwarming.

Overall, I've seen another side of Tilman and learned about his philanthropic causes. Tilman gives generously back to numerous charities and does a lot of good for people. He has been a great business partner and is not afraid to invest in good ideas.

Tilman is currently a partner in our T-REX and Yak & Yeti restaurants. I'm still disappointed about the sale of the Rainforest Cafe restaurants, but I now appreciate Tilman's strengths as a good restaurant operator—that he can save on costs, expand outlets, and improve the quality of the food and the consistency of the guest experience, all while making a profit. I've realized that I can disagree with some of his policies but still appreciate him as an astute businessperson.

Working together the second time around, Tilman and I have come to respect each other. He appreciates my creative talents, and I value him as an industrialist who runs complex businesses successfully and who had the courage to invest in my concepts when significant financial risk was involved. He certainly wasn't a bottom-feeder when he shelled out one hundred million dollars to invest in my restaurant concepts. Tilman stepped up to the plate and took a big chance on my ideas, and I owe him greatly for his faith in and financial backing of my projects.

Not only does my experience with Tilman underscore the value of giving someone another chance but also it illustrates the importance of never assuming you know someone completely, inside and out. In fact, by giving someone a second chance, you may be giving yourself a new business opportunity as well.

Steven and Tilman Fertitta at the Toyota Center watching the Houston Rockets vs. Minnesota Timberwolves basketball game on January 18th, 2018 in Houston, Texas.

I recall one particularly acrimonious business meeting where some nasty comments were exchanged along with some really biting insults. Nobody was going to budge; everyone was angry. The two investors I was speaking with said they wanted nothing more to do with me; the deal was off. They told me to leave. I did, but not permanently. I went to the bathroom, took about ten minutes to let everyone cool off (including myself), and walked back into the room. I gave one of the partners a hug and told him we were going to get this deal done and I was sorry for some of the things I had said.

What I learned that day reconfirmed my belief that ego can be a killer, especially an unchecked one. A current partner, Dick Portillo, offered me a deal. But he gave me only ten minutes to make up my mind. Being forced into a fast decision irritated me (even though we had been talking about this deal for a couple of months), so I said no. That was ego talking.

The next day, assuming that Dick was still interested in partnering, even though I had already missed my deadline and turned him down, I called him back and suggested we keep talking. We met on his yacht in Florida and closed the deal that same day.

Everyone deserves a second chance—it's all part of crossing a bridge carefully the next time around. And thank heavens we're given the opportunities, as many amazing things may never have occurred without them.

Dick Portillo and his high school sweetheart, Sharon, used the $1,100 they had saved to buy their first home to start a hot dog stand. In 1963, they opened The Dog House in Villa Park, a suburb of Chicago in a 6-by-12-foot trailer that had no bathroom or running water. By 1967, their Dog House had become a huge success. It grew into an empire, renamed Portillo's Hot Dogs, and was sold for a billion dollars in 2014.

Dick Portillo is now a partner in the Boathouse at Disney Springs in Orlando, Florida.

From left to right: John Barsella, Larry Shane, Karen Peterson, Patty Sullivan, Dick Portillo, Sharon Portillo, Steven Schussler, Steve Lombardo III, and Steve Lombardo Sr. celebrate their Boathouse partnership on Dick Portillo's 150-foot yacht in Naples, Florida.

SECTION V

PHILANTHROPY

CHAPTER 27

Entrepreneurial Social Responsibility

No one is useless in this world
who lightens the burden of another.

—Charles Dickens

Self-Examination Question:

Do you try to incorporate sustainability and socially responsible practices in your business?

One day, early in my entrepreneurial career, I remember listening to Bob Hope, who said, "If you haven't got any charity in your heart, you have the worst kind of heart trouble." I thought a lot about that comment. It made me realize there is more to life than simply making money. Sure, I believe that "getting" is important—but so is giving back. Some of my pragmatic friends might argue with me and say that the only goal of the entrepreneur should be financial gain. I disagree. To these pragmatists I would say that helping others while helping yourself is not counterproductive. Quite the opposite, in fact—it can even be synergistic. Thus, the old adage: "You can't help someone uphill without getting closer to the top yourself."

Some of my fondest entrepreneurial memories involve times I incorporated social responsibility into our business plan. For instance, when we were building our first Rainforest Cafe at the Mall of America, I decided to hire the homeless and give them jobs spraying fire retardant on the outside of artificial greenery (so it couldn't catch fire in the restaurant). My idea was to give them a chance to get off the streets and back on their feet. It was the kind of work where you didn't need to wear clean clothes or be immaculately groomed to get the work done.

I remember taking some of my staff and scouring areas under bridges and in abandoned buildings where the homeless congregated, in order to search our potential labor pool. The experience was humbling. When all was said and done, my attempt at social activism resulted in the good, the bad, and the ugly.

The "ugly" was the reality of what happens when you try to pull somebody off the streets. We were dealing with people who had drug and alcohol problems, some who stole, others who came in late or didn't show up at all. The "bad" was it cost us twice as much money to hire and train the homeless as it did our other workers. But the "good" involved the success stories: the homeless guys who left the streets and became productive, successful citizens.

One guy's name was Jim. He had been living on the street and in shelters before he worked with us. After his time with us, he ended up getting himself a steady job and his own apartment. He cut back on his drinking and reconnected with his family. Jim's story, and those like it, made all our efforts worthwhile. It cost our company money, but I'd do it again in a heartbeat.

Social responsibility is something that comes with the territory, particularly when your territory is an establishment that serves liquor.

Way back in the 1970s, when I was running JukeBox Saturday Night, we offered patrons who had too much to drink free rides home. This was long before most bars and nightclubs were offering such a service. We didn't have to do this, but I felt it was the right thing to do.

There were several ways we ensured that our intoxicated patrons didn't drive home. One approach involved selecting a designated driver. (Our DD program was recognized by the U.S. Department of Transportation as one of the top five programs of its type in the country.) If a group of people came into the club *together*, and one of the members was willing to abstain from drinking alcoholic beverages, he or she was given a special pin. That person was then served soft drinks on the house all night long so he or she could take his or her alcohol-consuming friends home safely. Another approach involved our doormen, who were trained to check out all patrons as they left the club. Our team members were required to complete an alcohol-awareness training course, and, using the evaluation techniques they learned, if they decided that somebody was too drunk to drive, the club paid for that person to get a taxi ride home.

Probably our most successful and expensive approach to keeping our drunk patrons from getting behind the wheel was based on some research we had conducted at JukeBox. We discovered that people didn't like to give their car keys to a stranger and then take a taxi home. The problem was that they woke up the next morning wondering what happened to their cars. So we instituted a program where we persuaded the patrons who were too drunk to drive to let us tow their cars to their homes. We spent about one hundred thousand dollars per year for two tow trucks, but it was worth it because it got us involved in the community and, most importantly, saved lives.

Our themed restaurants are also concerned with being socially responsible and encouraging respect for and conservation of the environment. In their early years, our Rainforest Cafes promoted a "rescue the rain forest" program. We contributed part of the restaurant's profits to environmental causes and sent our bird curators to local elementary and high schools to teach children about the beauty of the rain forests and how they were endangered and needed protection. Emphasizing sustainability and being "green" in our themed attractions are very important to me, and I work hard with my team to keep environmental awareness in the forefront of our minds. It is something all businesses need to do, and hopefully *will do,* in the years to come.

CHAPTER 28

The Importance of Entrepreneurial Philanthropy

We make a living by what we get;
we make a life by what we give.

—Winston Churchill

Self-Examination Question:

Do you believe it is important to give back to support charitable causes?

Booker T. Washington said it perfectly: "If you want to lift yourself up, lift up someone else." I can think of no better way to do this than through philanthropy. I truly believe a great award awaits the giver when it comes to undertaking philanthropic activity. When you invest your time, energy, or money in serving others, you will gain great dividends.

A doctor friend once told me about a scientific study conducted in the United States. It showed that regular volunteer work dramatically increased life expectancy. Men who did no volunteer work were two and a half times as likely to die during the study as men who volunteered once a week. I wasn't really sure I believed my friend until I read a book by Peter McWilliams entitled *You Can't Afford the Luxury of a Negative Thought*. According to the author, "Doing good for others enhances the immune system, lowers cholesterol, strengthens the heart, decreases chest pains, and reduces stress. A study at Harvard showed that even *thinking* about doing service produced positive psychological results." Maybe we should get involved in philanthropic activities as if our lives depended on it—they just might!

Do these findings come as a surprise? They shouldn't. Think of the times you have served others. Remember the good feelings you experienced? The joy of giving your time, service, or money to others is more than a noble calling; it is a pleasurable one. It is uplifting, a high without the need for drugs or alcohol. It is an affirmation of the human spirit. As humanitarians have long pointed out, "A man's true wealth is the good he does in this world."

When it comes to philanthropic work, I have long been an ardent supporter of one in particular. It was founded by an incredibly dedicated philanthropist, Kim Valentini, who gives amply of her time and inspiration to ensure its success. It is called Smile Network International and exists solely to help children from third-world countries who cannot afford medical services to receive surgeries to repair cleft palates and lips *free of charge*. Every penny raised for this charity goes directly to the costs of performing these life-changing surgeries. For five hundred dollars, doctors and nurses can fix the cleft palate or cleft lip of a child and put a smile on his or her face forever.

In the United States, we take such surgical miracles for granted. But in third-world countries, that just doesn't happen. And without surgical intervention, the child's life will never be the same. I have personally witnessed how kids with these facial disfigurements are treated. They are stared at, ridiculed, shunned. Many don't attend school; they're kept locked up at home because their families are embarrassed to have them seen in public. It is a life no person would want to, or should have to, endure.

Surgically repairing a child's facial disfigurement changes that child's life forever. To see the change is truly a blessing. I've worked in the hospitals where these medical miracles are performed. I've held the kids before and after the operations. And I've been there when the kids smile for the first time and their parents cry for pure joy. It is the most heartwarming experience you can possibly imagine.

I support Smile Network because I believe in it with all my body and soul. I take a portion of the money I earn from all my entrepreneurial activities, including this book, and donate it to Smile Network.

But my interest isn't focused exclusively on Smile Network. In the six years since this book was first published, we have found that our social responsibility has expanded to include multiple causes and charities. In fact, those charities and Smile Network will receive financial support from the proceeds of this updated book.

Broadening philanthropic interests makes perfect sense. As your professional success increases, you're naturally approached by others interested in your support. And, since you likely have financial means and professional contacts that you may not have had earlier in your career, it's natural that the scope of your social responsibility grows as well. It's not a matter of choosing this cause over that one—rather that you have the ability to be even more involved with a broad array of valuable activities.

Giving back does not have to be just through money. If you are rich in talent and time, volunteer. There are a multitude of organizations that you can help. A kind gesture or encouraging word can help ease pain. I am often asked to speak at nonprofit organizations about innovation, sales, marketing, and creativity. When they do not have the budget, I will make every effort to help them at no cost.

It is a noble calling to share with the less fortunate a portion of what you have earned. It is something we can all do to change the world for the better and, in the process, ourselves as well. For as Albert Pike so eloquently reminds us, "What we have done for ourselves alone dies with us; what we have done for others and the world remains and is immortal."

Smile Network International founder Kim Valentini with Steve, a founding member, at a Smile Network event in Minneapolis, Minnesota.

SECTION VI

NEW INSIGHTS

CHAPTER 29

Labor of Love

Great works are performed not
by strength but by perseverance.

—Samuel Johnson

Self-Examination Question:

Would you continue to pursue a project that faced opposition?

Inspiration can strike at most any time.

Believe me, I know. In the case of one of my most personally rewarding projects, it came when I was sitting on the toilet.

I was in the bathroom reading the August 18, 2010, edition of the *Minneapolis Star Tribune.* One article in particular caught my attention: "Will a Bidder Save EP Barn?"

The story was about a barn in Eden Prairie, Minnesota, not far from my home. Built in 1942, the Goodrich-Ramus barn has a classic arch roof design and occupies 6,400 square feet. The oldest standing barn in Eden Prairie, it's listed as a national historic site, reminiscent of the sort of dairy barns that once filled the area.

But the barn faced problems on all sides. Since it was situated along the planned expansion of a forty-seven-mile hiking and snowmobiling trail, many local officials thought the best thing to do was just tear it down. That would have been fine with officials from a nearby airport, who, along with the Minneapolis Airport Commission, considered the barn an aviation hazard.

Contributing to the ruckus on the other side of the argument, many people who loved the barn wanted to save it, especially those from various historical societies who insisted that the barn be retained in its current form.

As it happened, I was looking to buy a building. I needed a place to store my motorcycle and car collection that I use as props when I'm working on new ideas and projects—my creative "laboratory."

The article said the minimum bid to buy the barn was sixty thousand. All bids were to be closed. I immediately called my attorney, Tom Zappia, and told him I wanted to buy it.

"Well, have you seen it yet?" Tom asked.

"No, I'm sitting on the toilet!" I answered, tempted to pull the lever to underscore my point. "I just read this article. It would be perfect for me."

"Well, I strongly suggest you go look at it first."

I did.

And literally fell through the floor of the great room loft on the upper level. The floor of the wooden structure had rotted from years and years of neglect.

Only the part of my body you don't talk about in polite company stopped me from going all the way down.

Like the floor, the place was pretty much a complete wreck. I could see why so many people wanted it torn down. But, looking past its current condition, I could also see its great bones. It could be another Schussler Creative Laboratory that would house all my cars, motorcycles, and props. I freaked out with excitement.

I called my attorney back and told him to put in a bid. He agreed to submit the minimum sixty thousand dollars.

The next day I found out that 450 people had looked at the barn. Worried that I might lose out, I called my attorney again, and we agreed to substantially boost my bid to eighty thousand.

I called him again the day after.

"I've talked to you more in the last three days than in the past six months," Tom quipped.

"I want to change the bid," I told him.

"You need a doctor, not a new bid," he shot back. Worried about losing the barn, I told him to increase the bid to $82,000. He agreed.

A month went by. To be honest, by that time I had forgotten all about the barn. Then, at 11 p.m. on September 16, 2010, my phone rang. It was Laurie Blake, the lady who had written the article in the *Star Tribune* newspaper about the barn's demise.

"I'm calling to congratulate you as the new owner of the Goodrich-Ramus barn in Eden Prairie," she said.

"Thank you so much, but may I ask what you are talking about?" I asked.

"The governmental agencies just met, and you won the bid," she explained. "You're the new owner of the barn!"

"Fantastic!" I practically shouted into the phone.

"Well, wait: before you get off the phone, there's something else you should know."

"What's that?"

"You were the only bidder."

So, as it turns out, I paid a little more than necessary, having bid against myself twice, but I was thrilled to have the barn that I wanted.

And, like the old saying goes, be careful what you ask for, because you just might get it.

I came to find out later that no one else had submitted a bid because the barn came with so many restrictions. These had scared everybody away because they made it difficult to use the barn for anything other than storage. Since the barn was a historic site, it had all kinds of easements and limitations as to what you could and couldn't do to the existing structure. There were numerous restrictions from many government agencies, including the Federal Aviation Administration, which wanted to put a red blinking light on the silo to make sure planes could see it.

Green Acres Event Center, an Enchanting Event Center in a Historic Barn™, is the first and only event center in Eden Prairie, Minnesota.

Steven and Sunhi Ryan-Schussler with the 2012 Barn of the Year Award. The award was given by Friends of Minnesota Barns for Best Non-Agricultural Adaptive Re-use of a historic dairy barn.

It went on and on and on. And to purchase it, I, as the buyer, had to sign all these agreements saying that it would never be used for anything other than storage. I signed them. And I bought the barn. But, nobody said anything about a white picket fence. Or colorful fiberglass cows.

So I installed a pretty white picket fence around the property. And, as a tribute to the barn's original purpose as a dairy barn, I added fifteen eclectic fiberglass cows—painted as a baseball player, the New York City skyline and Picasso (PiCOWso), among others—shipped from the Philippines. After all, what's a dairy barn without a fence and cows?

Then the excitement started.

We started getting phone calls and letters daily from people in the community thanking us for saving their barn.

Their barn. You could see their attachment to the barn in an instant. People told us how it brightened their day, how we had made them smile as they passed it on their drive to work, enjoying the brightly painted cows and pretty picket fence.

That led to a community campaign of people asking us whether their son or daughter could get married there. People suggested we host bar and bat mitzvahs, confirmations, and "Sweet 16" parties. We even got a call from the leaders of a nearby church asking whether they could hold a dance in the barn (they wanted to serve beer, but alcohol was prohibited in the church itself!).

Then came a letter from the wife of a bank president. Why, she asked, didn't we turn the barn into an event center?

That was the jump start. We approached the city and asked whether officials would consider rezoning the property, changing it into an event center that could be enjoyed by countless numbers of people.

Two and a half years later, the barn, renamed Green Acres Event Center, opened on March 1, 2013, the first and only event center in Eden Prairie. The renovation years were crowded with enormous obstacles and challenges. It seemed like there were thousands of them.

One was the construction work itself, with everybody in the city and state watching us. The roof of the barn alone, which required some twenty workers and an intricate system of scaffolding, took close to a year to install. We installed crystal chandeliers that were given to us by Steve Sopczak III. We brought in jukeboxes from my old JukeBox Saturday Night club for ambient lighting. Every single light in the entire place could be dimmed to set any mood you wanted.

The silo was turned into a wine cellar. We bought an old cigar store Indian and installed it with a garage door opener. Push a button, and the Indian door rose, revealing a wine cellar with a forty-five-foot-high ceiling illuminated by a crystal chandelier. This intimate space is decorated with a wine barrel table, hardwood floors, a fireplace, and the barn's original brick walls made from yellow baked clay.

Because there were only five parking spots, we bought a drainage pond from the city that was almost two acres in size and converted it into a brightly lit parking lot. (When we bought the pond from the government, we also built a new drainage pond in return.) We even installed our own fire hydrant.

Of course, none of this could have happened without all sorts of necessary forms of approval. After an intensive push that took two years, we were able to have the property rezoned from agricultural to commercial. We partnered with Paul Dzubnar and his Hightop

Hospitality company, which specializes in award-winning catering and restaurants. We argued with the national and state historic societies that objected to the parking lot and the new lighting. They even wanted us to keep the original windows, even though they were cracked and broken. We also had to put in a set of stairs for the third time because the existing set was a mere quarter inch off and failed to meet safety guidelines.

But, we handled the challenges as they inevitably popped up. Terry Enstad, the city's building department inspector who required us to have the stairs torn out and replaced, actually came out with his tools on the weekend and helped us install the new stairs, even adding lights to them.

The first time I met Terry, I bought pizza for all the guys working that day.

"I'm not allowed to do this," Terry said.

"What's that?" I asked.

"Accept gifts."

I looked him squarely in the eye. "You're telling me you're not allowed to sit down and have a slice of pizza to discuss my project with me? I'm not buying you a Ferrari; I'm buying you a slice of pizza! I know the rules. You can't accept anything over five dollars."

Now it was his turn to stare. "How would you know that?"

I grinned. "I looked it up before I bought the pizza."

He laughed. "You know," he said, "I've never encountered someone like you before in my entire life."

That may have been the single best slice of pizza I ever had, even though I didn't take a single bite!

Overall, we had to go through more than fifteen governmental agencies of all sorts, fighting for every single thing that we wanted to do (there's a partial list at the end of this chapter). But the more resistance we got, the more we responded with greater enthusiasm and creativity.

Especially on opening night.

We opened the barn in 2013 with a party for several hundred people. We had valet parking outside, with hundreds of cars lined up to move cars to our friends' lot at Elliot and Hummingbird Aviation, because we had not yet built a new parking lot. The place was absolutely jammed. At six o'clock, a twelve-piece orchestra started to play.

At 6:20, just as the band finished its third song, all the lights went out.

I mean out, gone, done, black as midnight. The transformer on the street that provided electricity to the building had blown up.

As our team scrambled to light candles all over the place, I got on the stage with a megaphone. After quieting everybody down, I explained that we didn't know what the problem was.

"But," I went on, "there's good news and bad news."

"What's the good news?" the crowd shouted back.

"The good news is the party continues. The bad news is you're going to have to look a little bit harder to see the person you'd like to dance with!"

And with that, the band started performing a cappella. People were dancing, eating, drinking, and enjoying themselves as though nothing was the least bit unusual. We built fires on the outside of the building and brought even more candles inside. Guests later said it was the best party they'd ever been to. Many stayed until one o'clock in the morning.

We had turned a potentially huge disaster into the most amazing, joyful, and memorable event possible. Dimly lit, the party was sultry and mysterious—an event that guests still talk about today. Some even believe the candlelit party was intentional! It was a model of reacting fast in a positive manner and turning lemons into lemonade.

Of course, the electric company dispatched repair trucks, but they were not able to restore the electricity at the party. We gave the repair guys food, and, in talking with one of the engineers who came out, we found that the outage had been caused by an improperly sized transformer that the electric company itself had installed.

But it didn't matter. Guests later said it was the best party they'd ever been to. Many stayed until one o'clock in the morning. To top it off, the electric error was documented in writing. Later, I talked with company officials and explained how they had been responsible. They wrote us a check for food and drinks, the entertainment, staging, and even my time!

We had turned a potentially huge disaster into the most amazing, joyful, and memorable event possible. We now have close to one hundred events a year at Green Acres Event Center—thanks in no small part to the commitment and leadership of my wife, Sunhi Ryan-Schussler. People have their weddings there. They have parties there. They have happy memories and pictures that will last for their entire lifetimes. The guests' feedback has been along the lines of "best wedding and/or party I have ever been to."

Green Acres has won all kinds of national awards, including entry in The Knot's Best of Weddings Hall of Fame, a world-renowned website for weddings; "Best Non-Agricultural Reuse of a Barn" by the Friends of Minnesota Barns; "Favorite Venue" by Minnesota Women's Press; and the ILEA's (International Live Events Association) 2016 Star Award. We received the 2016 Heritage Preservation Award, which recognizes an outstanding contribution to the rehabilitation, restoration, and use of Eden Prairie's heritage resources.

This restored barn is now a big part of the city's community. Grandfathers and grandmothers come, park on the side of the road, take their grandkids for a tour of the cows, and then take pictures next to them for their holiday cards.

When we have our lawn mowed, the city and the airport watch us with binoculars from the tower on the airport field. They then send out their trucks to mow the emergency landing field adjacent to the barn because they want it to look manicured for us.

It all started with a vision from the community and our passion to see what something could become that might be beneficial to all. We started work on the barn way before I had an actual business plan (something I don't advocate others doing!). But I was so in love with the idea, so enthusiastic and passionate about creating an event center for Eden Prairie, that I simply couldn't wait to get started.

Passion helped us overcome all the roadblocks and obstacles we ran up against.

The motivation to restore the barn was not to make money—I knew that would come in time.

The appeal of the project to me was universal—no one could come out a "loser" from transforming a crumbling barn into a standout event center. Going into the project, it was hard to imagine anyone opposing it.

An unfortunate fact of life is that no matter how wonderful a project may be, regardless of how many people stand to benefit, there will often be opposition. That can derive from professional objections to more personal ones—some people simply don't like things that make others happy or someone succeeding where they didn't.

The important thing to bear in mind is not to let opposition or roadblocks take you by surprise. They will always exist. And, rather than being rocked back on your heels in shock—*How could anyone have a problem with something so wonderful?*—be ready for them. Anticipate and expect. Every time our team encountered a new form of opposition or objection, we simply redoubled our efforts with an even greater commitment to seeing the project through, never taking our eyes off the goal.

Every day, I approached everyone with a smile—those who were supporters of the project as well as those who opposed it. A lot of people didn't want to talk to me and thought my barn in Eden Prairie wasn't important enough to take their time.

But we stuck to our guns. We made numerous appointments with people so the barn would stay on their radar. When some people didn't return phone calls, I kept calling because, to me, a no is simply a yes waiting to happen (as I referenced in Chapter 17). Show your commitment and let those who can help you know that no matter what, you're not going to stop.

There were more than fifteen different agencies and organizations that had to give approval for Green Acres Event Center. To give you a feel for the sort of challenges that any project can face—even those that it would seem no one would have even the slightest problem with—here's just a partial list:

- Minnesota Department of Transportation
- Minnesota Historical Society
- Eden Prairie Historical Society
- State of Minnesota
- Hennepin County
- Metropolitan Airports Commission
- City of Eden Prairie
- Department of Maintenance
- Streets and Sanitation
- Eden Prairie Planning Department
- Federal Aviation Administration
- Eden Prairie Parks and Recreation
- Department of Natural Resources
- Xcel Energy
- Xfinity/Comcast

Happily, we also had a lot of folks on our side. We would like to express our appreciation and gratitude to:

- Nancy Tyra-Lukens, Mayor, City of Eden Prairie
- Ron Case, Council Member, City of Eden Prairie
- Kathie Case, President, Eden Prairie Historical Society
- Robert Erickson, Sr. Development Associate, Wildamere
- Terry Enstad, City Inspector, City of Eden Prairie
- Kevin Schmieg, Building Official, City of Eden Prairie
- Jim Smart, President, Smart Associates
- Jeff Hamiel, Executive Director, MSP Metropolitan Airports Commission
- Dennis W. Schulstad, Council Member, City of Minneapolis
- Jeff Nawrocki, Assistant Director of Facilities, MSP Metropolitan Airports Commission
- Mike Franzen, City Planner, City of Eden Prairie
- Nick Peterson, Sr. Engineer, Hennepin County
- Brad Aho, Council Member, City of Eden Prairie
- Dennis Doyle, [former] CEO Welsh Companies
- Steve Durham, City Planner, City of Eden Prairie
- Tina Eide, Support Services, City of Eden Prairie
- Robert Ellis, Public Works Director, City of Eden Prairie
- Tim Fadden, Building Inspector, City of Eden Prairie
- Rick Getschow, City Manager, City of Eden Prairie
- Scott Kipp, Heritage Preservation Commission, City of Eden Prairie
- Julie Klima, City Planner, City of Eden Prairie
- Mary Krause, Sr. Project Engineer, City of Eden Prairie
- Dave Lindahl, Economic Development Manager, City of Eden Prairie
- Jay Lotthammer, Director of Parks and Recreation, City of Eden Prairie

- Kathy Nelson, Council Member, City of Eden Prairie
- Rodney Rue, City Engineer, City of Eden Prairie
- Chuck Schaitberger, Fire Inspector, City of Eden Prairie
- Steve Sinell, City Assessor, City of Eden Prairie
- Wendell Stockwell, Plumbing Inspector, City of Eden Prairie
- Jim Morrow, Lieutenant, City of Eden Prairie Police
- Robert L. Reynolds, Police Chief, City of Eden Prairie
- Matt Sackett, Sergeant, City of Eden Prairie Police
- Pete Vosbeek, Sergeant, City of Eden Prairie Police
- Christy Weigel, Licensing Technician, City of Eden Prairie Police
- Sherry Butcher Wickstrom, Council Member, City of Eden Prairie
- Grace Church Eden Prairie, Parishioners, Clergy, and Elders
- Elliot Aviation, Owners, Executives, and Employees
- Hummingbird Aviation, Owners, Executives, and Employees
- Chris Cooper, President, Hummingbird Aviation

CHAPTER 30

Friends Who Let You Bend and Break the Rules

There are small ships and there are big ships,
but the best ships of all are friendships.™

—Schussler Creative, Inc.

Self-Examination Question:

When friends and colleagues do not see business ideas through the same lens as you, do you take a friend or foe mindset? Do you have the wherewithal to continue the relationship, taking the time and effort to reach compromise or try to change their minds?

Sometimes, the very best ideas grow from other ideas that, when first suggested, were less than a rousing success.

Those of us of a certain age may remember Amphicars (discussed earlier in Chapter 9). These amphibious cars were introduced at the New York World's Fair in 1961. From 1962 to 1967, several thousand Amphicars were manufactured.

With an unassuming design that looked like an ordinary vehicle, they operated on land just like any normal car—that is, until they came to a pond or lake, at which point they became amphibious and could continue right into the water driven by propellers mounted at the back.

In 2011, I happened to see an Amphicar in a lake not far from my home. It had a retro look, reminiscent of a time when whitewalls, large fins, and pastel colors were all the rage. Although it wasn't particularly dramatic, the reaction it was getting from the people who lined the banks of Lake Minnetonka was a spectacle. People were smiling, laughing, and charging down to the water's edge to take pictures, myself included. Seeing this cute little car with its headlights barely peering over the water's edge gave me a rush. I smiled so hard it made my face hurt.

"Wow," I said to myself, "I need to learn more about this Amphicar."

One day, I was reading the newspaper and saw one of these novelty cars for sale. I snatched it up and immediately fell in love with its spirit of fun and interesting history. I discovered that two U.S. presidents, Lyndon B. Johnson and Jimmy Carter, owned Amphicars and enjoyed entertaining unsuspecting guests with them. Johnson was known to give visitors a tour of his Texas ranch in his Amphicar and suddenly drive into a lake on his property, all the while yelling that the brakes had gone out. Carter's reputation for practical jokes was similar.

The Amphicars came with a lot of problems, making them more unreliable as an everyday car. Yet, they were produced in an era where many families had only one car. Because of its impracticality, the Amphicar was more of a recreational vehicle and only used for a couple of hours on the weekend for fun—essentially, a large toy.

Most people couldn't afford this added expense and luxury item. They simply weren't made very well, with many aspects of the engineering suspect. Maneuverability on both land and water was poor. The engine ran so hot that passengers would sweat like crazy from the radiant heat. The heat caused vapor lock on the engine and carburetor, making it virtually unreliable on the water, especially after a long ride on the road. As one owner at the time summarized it, "It's not a very good car, and it's not a very good boat." Less than a ringing endorsement.

Only 3,200 were sold, and, by the time I became interested in them, there were at most 350 remaining. The rest were at the bottom of various bodies of water (many people did not close the door correctly or simply forgot to add the plug before entering the lake).

Still, I was hooked and bought a second and then a third Amphicar. Working with my friend Dave Flom—a master electrician, engineer, and mechanic, and a genius in his own right with more than twenty patents to his name—we learned everything we could about them. Enamored with their nostalgic and quirky appeal, we diligently researched all the mechanical and design issues. The more we learned, the more problems we discovered, but this only increased our enthusiasm. Soon it became an obsession for the both of us.

Along with the personal appeal of the cars, there was something else. At the time, we were in negotiations with the Disney Company regarding the construction of a new restaurant in the Orlando theme park. Since the location was on the waterfront of Disney Springs, I suggested naming it the Boathouse. It would be very upscale, serving top-of-the-line steaks, chops, and seafood.

In studying the location, it occurred to me that the prior use of the area hadn't taken advantage of the lakefront setting. The waterfront was not activated to make the most of its appeal. So, as part of my pitch, I proposed that the restaurant include rides in these amphibious cars. For me, the connection was obvious—the Amphicars would be the distinguishing attraction, providing a uniquely nostalgic, fun experience that would appeal to families and people of all ages.

In my excitement, I told them this new concept might be the most successful idea I had ever devised—one that would make the Boathouse stand out by having the only Amphicar ride in the world, an idea bigger and better than Rainforest Cafe, T-REX, and Yak & Yeti combined.

The Disney people went out of their way to be as diplomatic as possible about their Amphicar apprehension. They were completely on board with the idea of the Boathouse restaurant but did not totally understand the Amphicars. For one thing, they said they had no interest in making the waterfront into something more than it already was. And, as some Disney executives put it, the Amphicars looked like regular cars that were already halfway headed toward the bottom. From their point of view, one Titanic was enough.

Others, including Disney Imagineering, thought it was off-the-charts incredible. They only questioned the safety of the car and the ability of our team to deliver an out-of-this-world, uninterrupted water experience seven days a week, 365 days a year.

"Come on, Steve," they said with one voice. "Rainforest Cafe was a home run. T-REX was a home run. Yak & Yeti is off the planet. You're telling us that some short-lived fad from the sixties is going to be bigger than those?"

With the same hesitation, they turned down my Amphicar idea.

"Mind your own business," they told me. "You already have three concepts here, and in case you hadn't noticed, you don't own Disney."

Their no lasted for several years.

Having been in this position before, I told myself, as I discussed in Chapter 17, "No is just a yes waiting to happen." In my gut, I saw in full Technicolor that this idea could not fail—it was just a matter of being able to show others what I saw with absolute certainty.

I approached Keith Bradford, the vice president of Downtown Disney. Eager to put my idea of the Boathouse into a more tangible form, I asked him whether I could build a prototype to be placed in the Disney offices so everyone passing by would be able to see and take in all the special details. I told him all I needed was six hundred feet of space. I guaranteed that anyone who saw it would think it was the coolest thing ever. If they didn't, I promised I would pack up my stuff, slouch away with my tail between my legs, and never bother him again.

Keith balked at my request at first. Eventually, he asked me to make an architectural drawing of what I had in mind. I did just that. After he reviewed it, he cautiously agreed to give me the space I requested. "Okay, come build it, but realize one thing, Mr. Schussler," he said. "We have never done anything like this before, and we will probably never do anything like this again."

Flush with the sense of exhilaration you can get only when you feel the "rules" have been bent on your behalf, I hustled for the next three weeks. Every morning at 8 a.m. sharp, I was at the Disney offices with a crew of carpenters and electricians. In a flurry of activity, we assembled props, television sets, and more things than you could ever dream that could fit in six hundred feet of space. Finding the space limited to get my message across, I clipped and edited a video that had people saying Amphicars were the coolest, most imaginative things on the planet ("the best toy ever!"), eliminating all the criticism they had received.

I got so carried away that I found myself hauling out furniture, fixtures, file cabinets, and pictures off the wall, moving them into a huge truck in a nearby parking lot. In my enthusiasm, I ended up taking an extra six hundred feet—another slight transgression of the "rules."

I was so proud of my display. However, Keith had another reaction. He called me into his office with tears in his eyes. They were beet red as though he had been up all night.

"Are you out of your freaking mind?" he demanded, his voice shaking. "I don't know who think you are. I did you a big favor even though others did not want it. What do you do? You take over, moving our plants and file cabinets. I can't believe you even moved our operations into a truck in our parking lot! I'm so disappointed—I can't even begin to tell you how much.

"You took advantage of me!" He almost shouted the words. "I don't care if you have to stay here all night; you're going to take it down, every last bit."

I apologized and explained I was passionate about my idea and wanted him to see the Boathouse for what it could be. Realizing I may have gone too far, I agreed to dismantle everything. Keith, who had cooled down somewhat by then, allowed me to keep the display up overnight. He said I could start taking it apart the next day.

In my disappointment, I consoled myself with still having accomplished a couple of important goals. The presentation was beautiful. It captured every aspect of my idea. And, even though the Disney executives were less than thrilled at my commandeering far more space than I had been given, it made clear just how passionate I was about the idea. Nobody with less than complete and utter conviction in their concept would have been so presumptuous.

Those few hours of additional time changed the momentum in my favor. The next morning, a gentleman by the name of Wing Chao happened to walk through the Disney offices. At that time, he headed up Disney Imagineering and Creative worldwide. Mr. Chao and his team were incredibly detail-oriented, even to the point of making certain that every curb on Disney properties should be built at a certain height and angle. These were people who knew what signified Disney and what did not.

As Mr. Chao walked past with a group of other executives, the first thing they came across was my creation of the Boathouse attraction and retail restaurant.

"What in the world is all of this?" Mr. Chao asked.

"This is a new idea by Steve Schussler, creator of Rainforest Cafe, T-REX, and Yak & Yeti, to activate the waterfront," Keith replied.

Mr. Chao and his team took a few minutes to take in the Boathouse display and watch the accompanying video.

"This could work!" he declared suddenly.

Thanks to Mr. Chao's support, the display was allowed to stay in place for three full months.

Still, Disney executives kept insisting that they weren't interested in the Amphicars. Not only did they doubt the cars' safety and reliability but also they somehow thought they would detract from the high-end restaurant (particularly if one took a nosedive toward the bottom of the lake).

But I stood my ground, insisting that we couldn't do the Boathouse without the Amphicars. Thanks to prior work with concepts such as Rainforest Cafe and T-REX, I knew an attraction was a must. Top-of-the-line food and service aren't always everything; I knew that we needed something more to attract children—not just parents focused on a great meal.

The challenges to get approval for the Amphicars were enormous. Not only were we charged with transforming the cars into an attraction that was dependable, safe, and fun, but we had to meet the sky-high standards of Disney's engineering and safety people. But I was on top of that as well. Working with several prominent engineers, including one from Harvard, we essentially reinvented the cars. About 1,600 new parts were installed, including many components that hadn't been invented in the 1960s. These additions bolstered reliability and safety. The rear seat was moved back two inches to give passengers more comfort. Brand-new ignition and carburation systems were installed. The exhaust system was moved.

At Disney Springs in Orlando, Florida, Boathouse guests can view "floating pieces of artwork" right from the dock.

Steven's friend, celebrity chef Robert Irvine, takes his family for a spin in a '67 Amphicar while visiting the Boathouse at Disney Springs in Orlando, Florida.

A vintage Amphicar parked outside the front entrance of the Boathouse at Disney Springs in Orlando, Florida.

As a result, the engine's heat was trimmed by thirty degrees. Our Amphicars would no longer be floating saunas.

With our redesigned Amphicars, I decided, unannounced, to bring two of them to Disney and convinced the waterfront operators to let me put them in the lake. I then persuaded the reluctant Disney executives to take a ride with Dave Flom and me behind the wheel.

When the Amphicar splashed into the water and started its swim in the lake, their skepticism of four long years floated away in an instant. They flipped out and loved every second of the experience.

During their ride, they observed enormous crowds that formed, watching and taking photos. The executives said that they had never in their lifetime seen such an enthusiastic response from Disney guests. They now understood and appreciated the draw and attraction of these quirky cars.

Just as important, the Amphicars performed smoothly without the slightest mechanical issue. Not long thereafter, I got a phone message from Theron Skees, who is now the head of creative activities with the Disney cruise line.

"Hi, Steve, it's Theron Skees. I wanted to call with some very good news, if it hasn't reached you already. The Amphicar idea was accepted, and everybody was actually quite excited about it, so congratulations, my friend. Looks like we're on our way!"

But there was still a lot more work to be done. Consistent with their focus on absolute quality, Disney made it clear to us that the Amphicars had to be completely reliable. Even one day down for repairs was not acceptable.

To meet Disney's requirements, we selected six Amphicars, with two additional as backups, along with a safety vehicle in case anything goes wrong. At the end of each day, the cars would go to a full-time shop for a comprehensive inspection. After being serviced, they'd be brought back to the job before opening up the next morning. (To date, the Amphicars have never been down, with the exception of weather-related issues. They run seven days a week, twelve hours a day, with an average of sixty to ninety "swims" a day. The cars now have taken more than 33,000 trips and at a mile and a quarter per tour, they have, collectively, circled the world 1.25 times.)

We made the safety of our guests a top priority, producing a two-hundred-page manual with procedures for every mishap imaginable. How will a disabled car be picked up as quickly and efficiently as possible? What should we do if a person has a heart attack or someone falls into the water? How fast can we get someone back to land? What is our communication protocol? Do we call 911? We even practiced what to do if a hat or a watch goes overboard!

We also instituted an extensive training program for the captains operating the cars. They not only have to learn how to run the cars but also must be excellent swimmers. They are required to pass a demanding lifesaving test and be thoroughly knowledgeable about all safety procedures. The captains also look and act the part, dressed in crisp white uniforms complete with captain caps and epaulettes on their shoulders.

Turning the Amphicars around once they returned from a trip on the lake was a problem because there wasn't enough room on the ramp when the cars came out of the water. The solution we created was essentially a huge turntable built of concrete, a feature that we made into an attraction unto itself. As the cars rise from the water on the turntable, the captains groan, making a show of struggling to turn the big ship's wheel . . . all the while, merely pressing a button on the floor that mechanically turns the car around on the concrete circle.

Our overriding focus was on a guest experience that would be memorable and out of the ordinary, especially at Disney. Every hour on the hour, the captains assemble to perform a bugle call paying tribute to the American flag. At first, this created a new dilemma, as none of the captains knew how to play a bugle. Then we found a bugle that plays itself! The captains had a lot of fun learning how to perform as though they were actually playing it.

Unique elements like the bugle assembly helped the Boathouse appeal to every member of the family. But our planning couldn't end there. We had to find a restaurant operator that met Disney's high fine-dining standards. Since guests come in once for the "wow factor" and then come back again and again for quality food and service, we knew it had to be phenomenal. I initially discussed working with Dickie Brennan, a world-class restaurateur and owner of Brennan's, the famous restaurant operators in New Orleans, but the timing was not right for him.

During Thanksgiving, while my wife and I were in Chicago visiting family, we went to the famous Gibson's Bar and Steakhouse. We ran into the owner, Steve Lombardo Sr., a friend I have known for many years after having been introduced by Jimmy Rittenberg.

During that encounter, I invited Steve and Larry Shane, the CFO of Gibson's, to our laboratories and office in Minneapolis. I gave them a tour and then shared the overall concept of the Boathouse as a premier restaurant dining experience and a one-of-a-kind attraction that would be out of this world.

Like Disney, they were anything but convinced at first. In fact, in the middle of a meeting, they suddenly said they simply had too many doubts. No thanks, they told me. With that, they got up from their seats to leave.

"If you guys walk out of this room, you will be making one of the biggest mistakes of your life," I declared.

Steve and Larry looked at each other, shrugged, and sat back down. My evident passion about the project successfully delayed their snap decision.

We had a deal not long after that. The Boathouse is now a big success, honored as the number one restaurant in all of Disney properties out of more than five hundred, according to USA Today and People magazine. To this day, Steve and Larry laugh about how close they came to walking out. The food and service Gibson's provides at the Boathouse are second to none. The Gibson's Group is not only an outstanding team; they are now my partners and great friends.

How did the Boathouse idea that Disney questioned for five long years become one of the top-rated and top-grossing restaurants on Disney property? When it was just an idea in my mind, I saw clearly the Boathouse as it is standing today, down to every last detail. When others told me it wouldn't work, my belief in my vision stopped me from accepting no.

As mentioned in Chapter 17, no is yes waiting to happen. When Disney executives told me no, I stayed on course, maintaining my friendship with them. When the Gibson's Group turned down my idea, my passion drove me to speak up and convince them to reconsider.

It's hard to be patient and not let your ego take over, to not be hurt or angry when others are not supportive or stand in your way. When you have a creative idea that you believe in, do not be deterred from making your dream become a reality. At times, it is going to take every bit of strength and positive energy that you can muster to convince people, but never, ever give up!

It takes persistence and hard work to bring your creative idea and vision to life. Success is not achieved by doing just one big thing; it is the hundreds of little things that you achieve on a daily, monthly, and yearly basis. In our case, it took five long years. It took putting together a video featuring two American presidents having the time of their lives in an Amphicar. It took re-engineering a vehicle widely considered the worst car and worst boat ever built into one that was reliable and safe. It took writing a two-hundred-page safety manual. It took finding a bugle that could play itself. It took convincing Disney executives who had been saying no over and over for more than four years to hop in the Amphicars for a spin. It took standing our ground because we saw how the first and only commercially operated and captain-guided Amphicar tour in the world would make the restaurant a one-of-a- kind attraction.

The Boathouse, like Disney, needed to be family-oriented while being an upscale restaurant with an attraction, great food, and retail store. That's why, along with great food and service, I insisted on the Amphicars, the captains, the bugle assemblies, the fleet of dream boats on display, the floating dockside bar, and the "Boatique" retail store. Each element we added was a strategic way to appeal to all demographics.

Maintaining friendships and positive relationships are essential to success. Convincing people to believe in your idea after they have made up their mind against it takes persistence and passion. It is a lot easier to do when you have a solid foundation of friendship.

Introducing the Ducks

Entrepreneurs become energized by great ideas. That energy propels them to take an idea and build it into a workable form for others to see. Then comes the challenge of convincing others to come on board.

But there's another significant obstacle that entrepreneurs confront—one that, on the surface, may seem anything but a problem. The challenge is when others say your product is "good." And that good is good enough.

Not for me. I strive for great, fantastic, out of this world—not just good. Every one of my concepts has taken an average of five long years to move from an idea stage to reality. One reason is that, once I find something that I am passionate about, I stick with it even when I receive opposition from others.

After the thrill of convincing Disney executives of the enormous appeal of Amphicar rides as an essential attraction at the Boathouse, everything was smooth sailing . . . until I mentioned the retail store. Many of the Disney executives were adamant in their opposition to having a store at the restaurant.

"What high-end restaurant do you know of that has retail?" they asked.

"That's pretty funny," I answered. "Retail has been a part of Rainforest Cafe, T-REX, and Yak & Yeti."

Still, they resisted. To a certain degree, I understood why. Disney likes to have as much control as possible over every aspect of its theme parks, especially retail. Even though what we planned to sell at the Boathouse didn't conflict with other Disney items sold at the park, the executives still didn't like the idea of a retail component. If nothing else, they simply couldn't see a retail store being a significant part of the Boathouse, as though the two were completely unrelated.

Named the Boatique, the retail space I envisioned was reminiscent of the art deco period from 1939 to 1959—a time of glamorous movies stars, celebrities, and historical figures, such as Marilyn Monroe, Gidget, Humphrey Bogart, and the Kennedys, with an updated appeal for current consumer tastes. Consistent with an overall nautical theme, we planned to sell paddles and life preservers that could be customized with the buyer's name. We would also offer clothes, jewelry, gift cards, and more.

We were open to compromise. For instance, we initially wanted 2,400 square feet of space for the Boatique. Disney countered with 1,200. We decided we could live with that instead of endless wrangling.

The same was true with the "Oyster Girl," a neon figure of an attractive young lady dressed in shorts, a curve-hugging top, and hat. She was positioned over the bar. Some Disney folks said she was too—ahem—revealing. We quickly made her more modest by lengthening her shorts and raising the neckline of her top.

But that was not the issue that caused the most disruption. Rather, it was a small, inexpensive item that surprisingly grabbed the Disney executives' opposition: rubber ducks. And, for me, the cute, adorable ducks became an issue that I could not give up on.

"What are you talking about?" the Disney people demanded early on in our discussions. "You're not talking about ducks that are hanging in the window that have just been cooked, are you?" (At this point, they simply couldn't get past the idea of something being sold at the Boathouse that wasn't some sort of food item.)

No, we said. We're talking about little rubber ducks—the kind that children play with while taking a bath.

That didn't fly (or swim) in the least. The Disney folks felt that rubber ducks were simply out of sync for a restaurant serving top-of-the-line food. That, and they felt that simple rubber toys were equally out of place in a store that also sold twenty-thousand-dollar watches.

"You're not selling rubber ducks," they said flatly. And since they had final say on what we could and couldn't sell, they assumed that was the end of that.

I couldn't believe it. For one thing, the ducks were in keeping with the nautical feel of the entire restaurant and related attractions. I knew in my gut that the ducks would be appealing to a wide variety of demographics, from young children to doting grandparents. To me, the Disney mandate of no ducks seemed completely mystifying and arbitrary. It was a component that would add whimsy, fun, and so much more.

Needless to say, we had many meetings where we presented the benefits—even bringing in a bathtub to showcase how cute the ducks looked in water. A little motor was put in the water to generate a current so the ducks would swim in circles. The ducks may have been going in circles, but I knew I was not. I was determined that the ducks find a place in the Boatique.

After a four-year refrain of "no ducks," they finally relented. A Disney executive stood up in one particular meeting and announced, "I have no problem with ducks." Then, looking around the room, he added incredulously, "Why are we all even here?"

Their agreement was a lucky break. I was so convinced that the ducks had to be an integral part of the store that we had already placed manufacturing orders (we had been working with a dormant company to produce the ducks—we were that confident). We formally presented the ducks to the Disney executives only two days before we were set to open.

The Ducks Take Off

When the Disney executives agreed to the ducks in the Boatique, I offered a guarantee similar to the one I had made when trying to win them over to the idea of Amphicars.

"They'll be the highest-selling item that we have," I promised them. "And if they're not, I won't sell them ever again."

That's a guarantee that I was able to deliver. To date, we have sold more than thirty thousand ducks in the three years that the Boathouse has been open. Of these, fifty-five hundred are ducks that we personally designed.

Don't assume for an instant that these are just like any other rubber duck. For one thing, the Boatique offers sixty-two different kinds of ducks. The AmphiDuck, a duck riding in an Amphicar, is the number one seller. Second is Mr. QuackCraft, complete with captain's hat and epaulettes, which was also our creation. Others include

Duckhorn, Duckarina (the ballerina duck), and Mrs. QuackCraft (Mr. QuackCraft's better half, outfitted with a scarf and sunglasses).

But there's more to the ducks than just cute designs and characters. They're the only rubber ducks made that, when you toss them into the water, immediately float right side up. (Try that the next time you give your kid a bath!)

Our requirements are rigidly high. Of course, the paint can't contain lead and must resist peeling or chipping off. No part of the duck can fall off in any way. We spent enormous amounts of time researching the ducks, testing them, and taking them apart to make certain that they all met our stringent requirements.

We've won awards for our ducks. In 2015, we received the prestigious Dr. Toy's Award for best classic children's product. We also received the Family Choice Award in 2016 for the best in children's and parenting products.

Our ducks have become a phenomenon in and of themselves, similar to the Disney pins that guests collect and trade. Customers will come to the Boatique and buy as many as a dozen ducks at a time. It's so rewarding to see that these "rubba" ducks have become as successful and popular as we imagined them to be.

Develop, Advance, and Enhance

When you have something good, never make the mistake of assuming that's all it can be. Research and development are the driving force to always improve. If you de-emphasize research and development, you're effectively losing your best opportunity to get better.

In Chapter 11, I discussed the importance of constant improvements. In the three years the Boatique has been open, the ducks' original packaging has been changed. The duck display has been relocated three times. In moving the ducks around the store, we're able to better gauge how certain ducks sell and the level of interaction customers have with them—particularly children. We even made the duck display the perfect height for children so they could easily pick their favorite one. It's an ongoing commitment to make the ducks more appealing and more fun for everyone.

For me, every duck that goes home with a happy owner is testimony to the endless possibilities that are made real by a commitment to never, ever settle.

CHAPTER 31

Choosing Compatible and Complementary Partners

No one can whistle a symphony.
It takes a whole orchestra to play it.

—H.E. Luccock

Self-Examination Question:

What are specific attributes to look for in a partner?

You'll recall from Chapter 14 that many people think of entrepreneurs as lone wolves–solitary visionaries.

An idea may be entirely their own, but bringing that idea to life often needs the building and maintaining of good strategic partners.

In many cases, partners are an important source of the essential energy that pushes good ideas into the realm of great. A supportive partner can also help rejuvenate your own sense of passion and energy during those times when it can be all too tempting to say the heck with it and toss in the towel.

Still, there are a few entrepreneurs who don't have partners. That's because it's often not easy to find a partner who fits with both your project and your personality. It's a difficult and complicated process, both in terms of identifying suitable partners and in working effectively with them. That's why many beginning entrepreneurs don't have partners. From their point of view, it's seemingly easier to do without them.

But the right kind of partners can often prove to be the difference between an idea that succeeds and one that collapses—or, by the same token, an idea that becomes all that it can truly be rather than just second best.

Knowing what to look for in a partner is not an exact science. But I can offer some ideas and observations that have proven helpful in determining the professional and personal makeup of a terrific strategic partner.

What to Look For

What one person may find appealing in a partner may be utterly irrelevant to another. But I've compiled some strengths and abilities that I feel apply to any good partnership:

Integrity. One of the most important things in picking a partner is integrity. How do you gauge integrity? I do a lot of research on a potential partner, vetting him or her by calling friends and associates. A good measure is how that person is seen by others. My partner at the Boathouse, Steve Lombardo Sr., has Lombardo Lane, formerly the famous Rush Street, renamed after him, which is at the intersection of his restaurant Gibson's Bar and Steakhouse. When a person is revered enough by the public to receive that sort of honor, you can be certain that the person is someone of high integrity.

Gibson's Bar and Steakhouse has been consecutively honored as the best steakhouse in Chicago due to its exemplary customer service. For instance, a guest ordered cheesecake, which was not on the menu; Steve located a place near the restaurant that did have cheesecake and sent a waiter down to pick it up, served it, and did not charge the guest for it. To me, that shouts integrity, with complete commitment to customer service. A person of integrity always puts others ahead of him- or herself, treats everyone fairly and with respect, and can always be relied on to go the extra mile.

A Complementary Voice. It's always a plus when a partner sees what you see and can understand your thoughts and ideas without undue explanation. But that's not to say that you want a carbon copy of yourself, someone who marches in absolute lockstep. Rather, a suitable partner is someone who doesn't think in precisely the same way or with the same pattern of reasoning. In so doing, that person proves complementary to you; they can contribute strengths that you may lack and won't necessarily come to the same conclusions (or, if he or she does, won't necessarily get there in the same way that you did). A different perspective can enhance your ideas, vision, ability, and skills, not detract from or conflict with them.

An Active Listener. As you likely remember from many of the stories I've shared, some of our greatest successes have come after a no—often, a no that's been repeated for years. Although it can be frustrating to have to endure what you might see as stubbornness, the fact that someone is ultimately willing and able to change his or her mind is another sign of a good partner. That's a partner who listens, who's willing to reconsider and recognize that great ideas are not always obvious to everyone at first glance.

A Student and Teacher. By the same token, that partner is just as willing to share what he or she knows with you. Collaboration—of both teaching and learning—contributes to a partnership that benefits everyone. Information and insights are readily shared, and, as a result, everyone grows.

Friendship Outside of Partnership. A "good" partner who, in reality, can't stand the sight of you really makes no sense whatsoever. In looking for a solid partner, pay attention to whether he or she likes you and whether you return that affection. If there isn't a genuine friendship, then an effective partnership is rather unlikely. Similarly, if you don't like someone, you may not be fully committed to his or her success.

A Life of Balance. We've all known someone for whom work is everything—24/7, work comes first, second, and third, with everything else well in the distance. That person may be a professional dynamo but may not make the best partner. For one thing, as often as not, even the most energetic and committed work junkie is going to burn out at some point. We all have a tipping point at which everything simply shuts down. Further, if this person's only focus is work, what kind of perspective and feedback is he or she going to offer—something reasonable and balanced or extreme and perhaps even unhealthy? Successful entrepreneurs—and, for that matter, most successful people in general—know what it means to have moderation in their lives. They know that work is not the end-all—it's also about loving the people around you and taking time to have fun with them. After all, aren't those the people whom the hard work is supposed to benefit?

Take Your Time

As mentioned earlier, a trait that might appeal to one person in a partner might differ considerably from what someone else will find beneficial. What's important is identifying what you value in a partnership and evaluating potential partners with those parameters.

Picking a strategic partner should not be rushed. By taking things slowly and working with someone on different projects, you can evaluate that person's actions and reactions to different situations. Further, you can see how he or she responds to people as well as certain events, both pleasant and difficult.

Additionally, take some time to think about what could happen if your long-time partner is no longer in the picture. What could happen if he or she loses his or her position in an organization? What if that person retires? How would it affect the commitments and promises that person made to you? Prior to entering a partnership that involves a company or organization beyond just one person, try to gain a sense of how central that person is to your mutual project and, in turn, what could happen if he or she is no longer involved. Will that person's influence and commitment carry over to the organization as a whole?

A partner is not just someone with whom you work on a particular project—a partner may be the attorney who reviews the necessary paperwork or the finance professional who makes certain that all money matters are in order.

Above all, trust your gut when choosing partners. A successful entrepreneur knows all too well that what he or she feels and knows inside are what point him or her in the right direction. Listen to your inner voice when selecting partners so that your ideas and inspirations become the best that they can be.

Steven celebrates the opening of the Boathouse in Shanghai, China, with Jeffrey Katzenberg, former chairman of Walt Disney Studios (left), and Bob Iger, chairman of the board of Walt Disney World Resort.

Some Final Thoughts

No one can cheat you out of ultimate success but yourself.

—Ralph Waldo Emerson

Will you look back on life and say,
'I wish I had,' or 'I'm glad I did'?

—Zig Ziglar

Courage is not the absence of fear, but rather the judgment
that something else is more important than fear.

—Ambrose Redmoon

Stay positive, all other choices are
pointless punishments to your psyche.

—Joe Peterson

Think of giving not only as a duty but as a privilege.

—John D. Rockefeller

Details make perfection, and perfection is not a detail.

—Leonardo da Vinci

I'm not done yet.

—Steve Schussler

Steven and his mother, Gloria Palazzo, at the opening of Rainforest Cafe at Downtown Disney in Orlando, Florida.

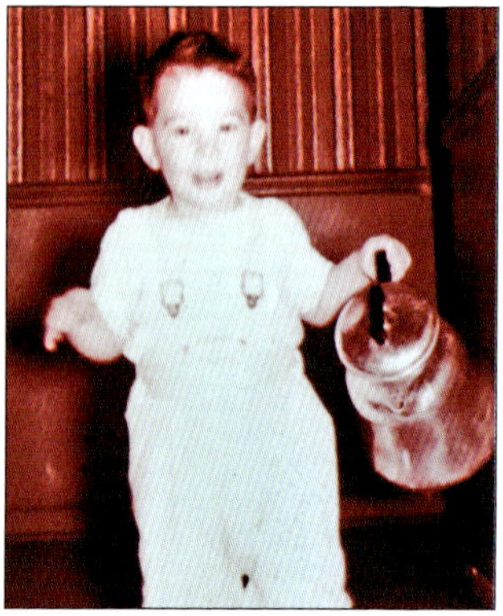

Steven's mother used to say that he was "training himself early for the restaurant business" with his favorite toy, the family's coffee pot.

Steven and family during a dinner for the Rainforest Cafe opening at Downtown Disney in Orlando, Florida. Back row, from left to right: Gloria Palazzo, Steven's mother; Steven Schussler; Jules Schussler, Steven's father; and Jason Schussler, Steven's nephew. Front row, from left to right: Robert Schussler and John Schussler, Steven's brothers.

Acknowledgments: No One Creates in a Vacuum

There are so many people to thank, so many stories, so much personal involvement by so many, that sometimes it's overwhelming to remember all of those responsible for my success. I probably could write a book just about all of you and how you have influenced my life. The best thing I can do is to continue with all of the beautiful life lessons I've learned from interacting with you and try to contribute back what you have given me. This book is not complete without my heartfelt thanks to the following:

My mother, Gloria Palazzo, who from the time I was eight years old worked to support me along with my two brothers, Robert and John. With my mother divorced and single, we moved out of a prosperous neighborhood and rather large home where we all had our own bedroom (I even had a brass bed) to a very modest second-floor apartment where my brothers and I shared a room. How she was able to pay for everything, take care of us, clean, cook, and work with three boys and no child support is beyond comprehension. After managing a couple gift shops in the Grand Canyon, my mother learned Spanish, entered the Peace Corps, and moved to Ecuador to work with its indigenous people. Retired now, she is stunningly beautiful and living in Lake Chapala, Mexico, outside of Guadalajara, an accomplished artist and writer still creating and experiencing life's adventures.

My dad, Jules Schussler, who died November 6, 2004, lived and retired in Las Vegas, Nevada. Dad tried very hard later in life to make up for the years of not seeing his family and not supporting my mother. He always enjoyed the action of craps and occasionally worked as an outspoken front man for a poker room in Las Vegas. Dad watched Lyle Berman play in the World Championship of Poker; his 3 a.m. phone call to me, telling me to grab a pen and write Lyle's name and number down, began my roller-coaster ride.

So my father was a salesman and my mother an artist—I guess I ended up with a little bit of both. I owe them gratitude for raising us the best they knew how. My brothers and I turned out great!

Sunhi Ryan-Schussler, whose love and affection, writing skills, and patience have made my life (and the lives of my family, friends, and Schussler Creative team) easier! I'm happy that I have found somebody who can handle my endless energy, multitasking, and sometimes hard-to-handle spirited personality. She is beautiful, inside and out.

My childhood best friend, Eddie Silverman, and his family—Diane, Joanne, Betty, and Marty—who owned Island Lake Camp in Starrucca, Pennsylvania, where I worked waiting tables and taught waterskiing to defray the cost of going to camp. I cannot tell you what amazing lessons you learn early in life living outside your own home.

My uncle Ted Comfort inspired me to lift weights and play football. A graduate of Harvard University, Ted was instrumental in my working at Silver Gull Beach Club and various other jobs I had growing up.

My teacher in high school, Mr. Dick Web, to whom I lost a bet in shop class—he actually cut my hair in class and then took me to a barber who couldn't fix it, so I ended up with a shaved head. Thanks too to Mr. Cohen, Mr. Miller, and Coach Jack Kershman, who also shared their passion for life and football with me.

My maternal grandfather, Bill Botwinik, who was always there with wisdom and financial support whether I asked for them or not. He would call, inspire, and send newspaper articles and books. I miss his daily lectures.

My brothers, Robert and John. God knows the three of us are very different! My younger brothers have supported my decisions and have always been there to pump me up.

My grandmother, Hennie, who lived in the Bronx, New York, would force my brothers and me to eat even after we finished a meal.

Dorothy and Benson Schussler, my aunt and uncle, were always there for me.

My cousins Martha and Frank Valladares and Sam and Norman Schussler played such an important part in my early years.

Jason Schussler, my nephew, son of my brother Robert, didn't quit and finished college after a long self-evaluation.

Brian Stone, from whom I learned such a great deal. We met at Vic Tanney gym, lifted weights together, ate steak tidbits, and had some cocktails. We became roommates, living in a penthouse together in Miami Beach, and I was fortunate enough to be best man at his wedding. His friendship and the interactions I had with him, his friends, and his family led me on my quest to be in the radio and broadcasting industry.

Steve Friedheim, my friend from Miami who died unexpectedly and too soon, encouraged me with his out-of-the-box thinking and never-accept-a-no attitude. He was so outrageous and incredibly generous. My love for tropical birds came from his interest in birds.

Dennis FitzSimons, my boss at Telerep in Chicago, where I was a rep for TV stations throughout the United States. He allowed me the freedom to grow as an entrepreneur and not be pigeonholed into thinking like everyone else. Dennis is the former chairman of the board and CEO of the Tribune Broadcasting Company, which owned WGN Television and the Chicago Cubs. I learned a tremendous amount from him.

Jimmy Rittenberg, who has saved my life on more than one occasion; he taught me the nightclub and restaurant business and gave me the opportunity to turn my retail store JukeBox Saturday Night into a chain of nightclubs/restaurants. Jimmy, whom I call Mr. Chicago, a.k.a. the Prince of Fun, is someone whose friendship, guidance, and tutelage I will always respect and be grateful for. He's like the character Jack Nicholson plays in the film *As Good as It Gets* who tells the waitress that she's made him a better person and a better man. That's how I feel about Jimmy.

Ernie Pesis owned the building where JukeBox Saturday Night was located in Minneapolis, Minnesota. His and his family's friendship and support gave me the freedom to build a network of friends and business associates that was such an important part in my life's journey.

Norm and Dorothy Pink, whose early financial support in JukeBox Saturday Night helped me when there were few other options. Thank you for including us in family gatherings and for being such great friends.

Tom Zappia is a world-class attorney, a caring family man, and a great friend. During a difficult time, he held up billing me for two years and continued working on my business with as much enthusiasm and attention to detail as he would give much larger-paying clients.

Lyle Berman, who provided the credibility and brought the financial team together to take my Rainforest Cafe idea from a dream to a reality. I'm so thankful Lyle took the time to talk to my father. Without Lyle there would have been no Rainforest Cafe, no T-REX, no Yak & Yeti. There are men who see mountains, there are men who climb mountains, but only a few men, like Lyle Berman, who move mountains. Lyle is a mountain mover.

"Famous" Dave Anderson, whose unselfish friendship and entrepreneurial spirit helped lead others to invest in Rainforest Cafe. Leading by example, he wrote the first check for half a million dollars to support the opening of the first Rainforest Cafe.

David Siegel. During the horrific 9/11 events, David and his team at Central Florida Investments allowed us to house our dinosaurs in the exhibit I created around T-REX in my quest to share the attraction, restaurant, and retail store with Disney. His generosity and support throughout the years have been amazing.

Herb Simon and his late brother Mel, the largest mall developers in the world, invested half a million dollars in tenant allowance money after visiting my home and taking the tour of the prototype of Rainforest Cafe. Herb and his family are visionaries who are not afraid to invest in entrepreneurial start-ups. You never forget who brought you to the dance.

Mel Simon, whose phone call discussing his investment in an animated dinosaur company led me on the quest to create T-REX, a Prehistoric Family Adventure, a Place to Eat, Shop, Explore, and Discover. Rest in Peace, Mel.

Bud Dare, whose early belief in me and in Rainforest Cafe paved the way for the opening of Rainforest Cafe at Walt Disney World and therefore provided our company with the opportunity to go public. I owe a great deal to him.

Rick Turnquist, who helped a great deal during the early years of Rainforest Cafe. He worked with tropical birds and had a great command of the English language; he was a spelling champion and walking encyclopedia. Thanks for all the help with the creation of Rainforest Cafe and for being a friend.

Doug Holod has been our corporate attorney for over twenty years and was instrumental in bringing Rainforest Cafe, T-REX, Yak & Yeti, Hot Dog Hall of Fame, and the Boathouse to fruition with his legal experience, expertise, professionalism, values, and integrity. Thank you, Doug, for your continued support, friendship, and camaraderie.

Dave Flom. What do you say about a guy who has played such a unique and vital role in all our projects? Amazingly multitalented, he has helped with breeding birds for Rainforest Cafe, working with animatronics for T-REX, rebuilding motorcycles for Backfire BBQ, re-engineering Amphicars for the Boathouse, and so much more. Thank you for your friendship, dedication, and hard work.

Jean Golden, a public relations and marketing guru, who graciously accepts change and is such a large part of our success.

The late Paul Ridgeway and the Ridgeway family, who always involved me in community events; they were responsible for putting on the World Championship Minnesota Twins ticker-tape victory parade and Curt Carlson's Christmas party. Paul and his family are committed friends and taught me the meaning of true friendship, as shown in bad times, not in good.

Tim and Jan Myslajek, whose family and friendship I cherish. Their support and that of Myslajek Accounting have been key in our planning and have played a key role in our success.

Dale Kivimaki and his family provided friendship, love, camaraderie, and resources for filming and capturing countless hours of our various projects at our laboratories without compensation.

Dan Lowe and Steve Graham, whose unselfishness and persistence brought T-REX and Backfire BBQ to the Legends at Village West in Kansas City, Kansas.

Maribeth Bisienere. Without her, T-REX, Yak & Yeti and the Boathouse would not have had a chance of being introduced to the Walt Disney family. She is one of the brightest businesspeople I've ever met. It is a privilege to work with her and I hope to continue to do so for life. She's a wonderfully talented, educated, fun, and incredible communicator, a woman with the highest of values and integrity. Her gifts just begin there and include having a great family and generously and graciously giving to her community and peers.

Maxine Clark, creator and former chairman of the board of Build-A-Bear, whose respect and friendship allowed us to become strategic partners in Build-A-Dino by Build-A-Bear, which today represents 50 percent of retail sales in the two T-REX stores we've opened.

Rich Melman, one of the world's top restaurateurs, who met with me endlessly during the early years of creating T-REX. At his Arizona home, we spent countless hours thinking of ways to make T-Rex a world-class attraction, restaurant, and retail store. I am indebted to him for his time, commitment, and friendship, both to me and to Smile Network International.

Nasser Kazeminy, the Kazeminy family, and the late John Goodman for without their love, support, and generosity we most certainly would not have achieved success in the opening of T-REX and Yak & Yeti. They provided funds to continue when finding suitable financial partners was difficult, never asking why, writing checks, and providing us the necessary seed money to see our projects through. Friendship is not a commodity that can be bought, sold, or traded. It's one of those things that you cherish, love, and appreciate.

In particular, I want to single out John Goodman, who passed away on March 20, 2016. I miss John every day and wish he were here to help us celebrate the successes that we have been able to achieve through his help and mentorship during difficult times.

Thank you, Tilman Fertitta, for having the courage and vision after buying Rainforest Cafe to invest in T-REX and Yak & Yeti. It's one thing to invest in Rainforest Cafe, a public company that opened forty-five locations on three continents. But it's something entirely different to invest in the Schussler Creative team and two unopened, unproven new restaurant/retail concepts after seeing them in our laboratories in Minneapolis. Your bold decision and support have millions of families enjoying great restaurant experiences. Also, congratulations on the purchase of the Houston Rockets basketball team and all your continued successes. I'm excited and happy for what lies ahead in our partnerships.

Thanks to Steve Lombardo Sr., Steve Lombardo III, Larry Shane, Bob Kanzler, John Coletta and John Colletti at the Gibsons Restaurant Group. Their integrity, exceptional quality of service, outstanding food, and high values have taken the Boathouse to an excellence that has exceeded my expectations.

Thanks to Dick Portillo and his team for their commitment to the Boathouse. Portillo is a model for how hard work, genuine care for others, tenacity, and steadfastness to providing quality food and service lead to success.

Kari Honoroff, who has put up with me for twenty-four years and counting—man, that's a long time—as my personal assistant, and I am proud that she has been able to handle every aspect of my life. She does so with dignity and grace. I am grateful to have had her as part of my team for so many years.

Thanks to Rae Olson, our senior vice president of retail and great friend, whose hard work, dedication, and upbeat attitude have been invaluable to our company. There is nothing she cannot handle.

Kim Anderson, who provided our company early on with fire retardant solutions to apply to our greenery so that the canopy I developed for Rainforest Cafe could pass health, fire, and building inspections. His tireless commitment to help us is appreciated and will never be forgotten.

Grace Gaffney, Nick Lehmann, and Kris Stewart, who are important members of our team. They bring new perspectives to every situation and face challenges with their youthful optimism. I'm grateful and honored to have them onboard, and I'm excited about the journey ahead of us.

The team at Schussler Creative: the term "team" takes on a whole new meaning when you think about the camaraderie and the escapades that we create on a daily basis. I cherish the time and the individual sacrifices that have been made by all of those with whom we work every day and those with whom we've come in contact over the years. Thank you for your undying support and loyalty.

Marvin Karlins, for his endless hours of dedication to the book and for the timeless energy he put into interviewing more than

150 people. He certainly has heard it all from the Steve Schussler stories he's had to endure.

Jeff Wuorio, who was recommended by the Jenkins Group to help me with the updating of this book. His patience, professionalism, and ability to be able to put up with our being late on a consistent basis are things that I will cherish forever. He's become a good friend.

Patrick Esposito, a flight attendant I met on a Delta Airlines flight to Las Vegas. Patrick's red tie was the same color red as the one being worn by the gorilla on the cover of this book. I was posing for my author photo that week and needed a tie of the same color. After sharing this with Patrick, I asked whether I could buy his tie. He said it was part of his regular uniform, so I then asked whether the tie was sold in a catalog. He replied that he couldn't wait to take it off, and while the other attendants laughed, he handed me the tie. Thanks, Patrick.

Tom Farrell, thank you for all your hard work and great legal advice. You're a great friend.

I would like to thank all of the unsung heroes who have not been named but have touched our lives and influenced us every day: the UPS and Federal Express drivers and mail carriers; the sanitation workers, police officers, and firefighters; the city, county, and federal government employees; the secretaries, executives, receptionists, truck drivers, and delivery people; and all of the professors and college students we speak with. Thank you for having influenced our lives and for having been part of our success.

A book of this type could not be written without the generous assistance and insights of dozens—actually, more than a hundred—helpful individuals. For the sake of brevity and fairness, we have included the names of these individuals in alphabetical order below.

Famous Dave Anderson, Steve's friend and mentor, was the first to write a check for the original Rainforest Cafe, which opened in 1994 at the Mall of America in Bloomington, Minnesota.

Steve wins the first annual Minneapolis/St. Paul Business Journal's 2017 Eureka! Innovation of the Year Award. Front row, from left to right: Jan Myslajek, Dave Flom, Sunhi Ryan-Schussler, Jean Golden, Steven Schussler, Kari Honoroff, Patrice Kullas, Jeff Golden, and Rae Olson. Back row, from left to right: Bob Hahn and Tim Myslajek.

If we have inadvertently left some names off the list, we deeply regret the oversight. To those of you whose names follow, thank you for all you have contributed to this project. We couldn't have done it without you!

Jeff Abraham, Susan Abramowitz, Cindy Abramovitz, Dino Adamidis, Vona Adamidis, George Aguel, Rachel Alde, Jeff Allison, Greg Alstad, Dave Anderson, Kim Anderson, Louie Anderson, Peggy Arthur, Douglas Bach, Charleen Bacigalupo, Gregory Bailey, Q (Quinton) Ballard, Mark Bartholomay, Scott Benjamin, Lyle Berman, Phil Bernard, Ted Bigos, Harry Billger, Sandra Billings, Maribeth Bisienere, Iris Blasi, Elizabeth Blau, Jack Blitch, Chrissy Bloemendal, Dave Bortner and fiance Michelle De Mist, Joe Bortz, William Botwinik, Dr. Barbara Bowers, Joyce Bowers, Bruce (Two Dogs) Bozsum, Keith Bradford, Robert Bram, Brooks Branch, Dickie Brennan, Ken Brimmer, Jeff Cantwell, Peter Caramalis, Greg Carey, Tate Carlson, Kathie Case, Ron Case, Bud Cataldo, Wing T. Chao, Jessie Chen, Kathy Chen, Dave Claflin, Maxine Clark, Jean Marie Clement, Jack Cohen, Michael Cohen, Stephen Cohen, Senator Norm Coleman, Michael Colglazier, John Coletta, John Colletti, Ted Comfort, Scott Conant, Tim Conklin, Joel Conner, Dean Constantine, Bill Cooper, David Cossetta, David Crabtree, Michael Crohn, Gary Crowder, Pat Cruzen, Megan Cullen, Cuningham Group, Dan Daddona, Carol Daniel, Bud Dare, Karen Daroff, Scott Darst, Brent Davies, Michael Davies, Alyn Davis, Brock Davis, Jillian DeKunder, Dayanny M. De La Cruz, Nicolas DeLarocque, Carlo Devito, Bob DiMarcantonio, Jon Donahue, Richard Dooley, Paul Douglas, Paul Dzubnar, Billy Ellis, Steve Engel, Terry Enstad, John Erickson, Patrick Esposito, Mitchell Grossinger Etess, Preston Evans, Thomas Farrell, Michael Fertitta, Paige Fertitta, Patrick Fertitta, Tilman Fertitta, Patrick Finnegan, Dennis FitzSimons,

Dave Flom, Jon Flor, Ric Florell, Ann Fontaine, Steven Frattalone, Mary Freidheim, Steve Freidheim, Grace Gaffney, David and Jan Gee, Michele Gendreau, Marge Gersich, Bob Getchell, Raphael Ghermezian, Jean Golden, Dr. Bob Goldman, Jannette Gonzales, John Goodman, Sid Goodman and the Goodman Group, Jon Gordon, Patrick Gottsch, Steve Graham, Juliet Grames, James Gravante, David Gray, Shelley Green, Clark Griffith, George Gross, Frank Grundhofer, Patricia Grundhofer, Jim Grzybowski, Kurt Hagen, Robert Hahn, Meredith Hale, Patrick Hamelet, Don Hamlin, Kevin Hammerbeck, Karmen Kelly Hanson, Heather Harford, Joan Harrington, Jeffrey Hartmann, Nick Hay, Penelope Haynes, Dennis Hays, Amos Heilicher, James Henke, Grandmother Hennie, Ryan Hickey, John Hinz, Doug Holod, Karl Holz, Kari Honoroff, Wissam Hourani, Dan Humphreys, Skip and Lee Humphrey, Lee Iacocca, Robert Iger, Robert Irvin, Mike Ivers, Gabriel Jabbour, Irwin Jacobs, Shelley Jacobs, Cheryl Johnson "C.J.", Hart Johnson, Randi Johnson, Terry Johnson, Tico Joing, Jim Jundt, Marcus Jundt, George Kalogridis, Bob Kanzler, Ambassador Sam Kaplan, Bill Kaplan, Erica Kaplan, Sylvia Kaplan, George Kalogridis, Marvin Karlins, Dan Kaufman, Nader Kazeminy, Nasser Kazeminy, Bill Keller, Pastor George Kenworthy, Coach Jack Kershman, Roberta Rose Kirschenbaum, Cynthia Kiser-Murphey, John Kitchener, Dale Kivimaki, Kona Grill Board of Directors, Wayne Kostroski, Jon Kramer, Jay Kreider, Brett Kroener, Maureen Kucera, Ray Kuik, Patrice Kullas, Leslie Kupchella, Rick Kupchella, Helmut Lange, Kevin Lansberry, Andy Lansing, Tony LaPlant, John Laub, Joe Lee, Patricia Lee, Nick Lehmann, Jay Leno, Dan Leonard, Justin Leonard, Don Lessem, David Letterman, Larry Levy, Paul Levy, Mike Lindell, Steve Lombardo, Sr., Steve Lombardo III, Jeanette Lomboy, Dan Lowe, Brett Machtig, Bill Mack, Debbie Mack, David Mackay, Harvey Mackay, Rebecca Maines, Magical Michael Makay, Rachel Maloney, Senator Bill Maravitz, Carol Marinovich, Abdul Hadi Fuad Mashal, Firas Mashal, Fouad Mashal, Moataz Mashal,

Mohamad Mashal, Samer Mashal, Jean McNeal, Jim McPhee, Bob Mecay, Richard Melman, George Meredith, Ron Meshbesher, Debrah Miceli, Elizabeth Mihaltse, Alan Miller, Coach Jake Miller, Wayne Mills, Warren Mitchell, Ted Mondale, Vice President Walter Mondale, Lafayette Montgomery, Frank Motter, Bill Murray, Tim and Jan Myslajek, Myslajek LTD, Dee Nolting, Charles Nurnberg, Martin O'Dowd, Doug Olson, Rae Olson, Paul Omodt, Lisa Onopa, David Page, Gloria Palazzo, Gary Parendo, Ron Pastore, Governor Tim Pawlenty, Ruben Perez, Megan Perritt, Ernie Pesis, Jimmy Pesis, Dan Peterka, Bill Peters, Karan Peters, Suzi Petersen, Bryce Peterson, Andrea Phillips, Michael Pierce, Joe Pine, Norm and Dorothy Pink, Paige Polinsky, Bill Pope, Dick Portillo, John Provo, Joe Puliafico, Dick Ragatz, Jill Ragatz, Mayor Joe Reardon, Scott Rehorn, Andy Revella, Craig Rice, Tony Rice, Paul Ridgeway, Paul Ridgeway, Sr., Roz Ridgeway, John Rimarcik, Jimmy Rittenberg, Steve Roach, Mark Robinow, Charlie Robinson, David Rockwell, David and Diane Rogers, Joe Rohde, Gregory Rothweiler, Steven Ruffner, Carlos and Ann Rullan, Tony and Linda Rullan, Debra Ruth, Lynda Ryan, Patrick Ryan, Sunhi Ryan-Schussler, Minneapolis Mayor R. T. Rybak, Ricardo Sanchez, Glenn Sands, Maria Elaina Santiago, Ed Sarquis, Elizabeth Sarquis, Steven Scheinthal, Jim Schemel, Lyla Schemel, Bill Schultz, David Schultz, Dorothy and Benson Schussler, Jason Schussler, John Schussler, Jules Schussler, Norm Schussler, Robert Schussler, Sam Schussler, Heidi Schweitzer, Mike Schweitzer, Marcia Seligman, Joe Senser, Ira Seret, Larry Shane, Linda Shaw, Tony Shaw, David Shea and the Shea Architect team, Marty Sherman, David Siegel, Larry Siegel, Stacey Siegel, Martin Silverberg, Eddie Silverman, Marty Silverman, Herb Simon, Matt Simon, Mel Simon, Theron Skees, Tom Sklar, Jim Smart, Jaye Snyder, David Solner, Bobbie Soper, Richard Stanek, Laura and David Starr, Rob Steinberg, Kris Stewart, Jay Stieber, David Stofcik, Brian and Penney Stone, Michael Tabman, Pat Tapp, Stan Taube, Richard Tettamant, Paul Teutul, Jr., Paul Teutul, Sr., Charlie Theros, Jim Theros,

Isaac Tigrett, Steve Torberg, Michael Townsend, President Donald Trump, Philip Turner, Rick Turnquist, Marvis Tutiah, Ercu Ucan, Valladaras family, Nick Valenti, David Valentini, Kim Valentini, Rocco Valentino, Martha and Frank Valladares, Dean Vlahos, Jeff Wagner, Todd Walker, Richard Wallace, Joel Waller, Pat Wannarka, Ned Waters, Dick Web, Al Weiss, John Wheeler, Jeffrey Wirth, Drew Wood, Doris Woodward, Kamala Young, Tom Zappia, Al Zelickson, Sue Zelickson, Rabbi Marcia Zimmerman

In memory of those who have passed since the writing of the first edition of this book:

Dean Constantine, Bill Cooper, Steve Freidheim, John Goodman, Sidney Goodman, Bill Kaplan, Ron Meshbesher, Leslie Pearlman, Paul Ridgeway, Sr., Jim Schemel

APPENDICES

APPENDIX A

Schussler Creative Inc. Mission Statement

Inventions, Ideas, Contraptions, and Dreams!

Schussler Creative is an innovative team that embraces imagination and creates theatrical hospitality venues, attractions, and experiences unlike any other!

Passion and imagination are two of the most powerful engines of success! At Schussler Creative, the paths of free-thinking individuals cross each other. Unusual and natural talents are used in an open forum to bring collective, creative ideas to fruition. When this occurs, opportunities arise that pave the way for phenomenal events.

The environment necessary for this to happen is simple: uncompromising standards to enhance the guests' experiences and a working atmosphere that encourages creativity.

Only those who risk going too far can possibly find out how far they can go!

APPENDIX B

The Entrepreneur's Credo

I do not choose to be a common man.

It is my right to be uncommon—if I can. I seek opportunity—not security. I do not wish to be a kept citizen, humbled and dulled by having the state look after me.

I want to take the calculated risk; to dream and to build, to fail and succeed.

I refuse to barter incentive for a dole; I prefer the challenges of life to the guaranteed existence; the thrill of fulfillment to the stale calm of Utopia.

I will not trade freedom for beneficence nor my dignity for a handout. I will never cower before any master nor bend to any threat.

It is my heritage to stand erect, proud, and unafraid; to think and act for myself; to enjoy the benefit of my creations and to face the world boldly and say: This, with God's help, I have done.

All this is what it means to be an Entrepreneur.

Adapted from "An American's Creed," an essay by Dean Alfange, which first appeared in the early 1950s.

APPENDIX C

The Artist's Credo

BY DOUGLAS BLOCH

To receive the inspiration to create, to share that creation with others, and to be totally supported in the process.

An inspiration that calls us to create. Once the inspiration is received, then we can bring that vision into the world as a song, painting, book, invention, new business, or any other tangible form.

After the creation is born, it needs to be shared with others. No one creates in a vacuum. It is only when the vision is successfully communicated to its intended audience that it truly comes alive.

The artist needs to be supported for what he does. If he has made a positive connection with his audience, the support will come—financially and emotionally. While it may not always be there immediately, it will ultimately arrive. This is where the artist needs to trust and be patient.

This dream is not just the artist's dream. It is our dream as well. Through work or play, job or family, vacation or avocation, you can experience the joy of creating, sharing, and being acknowledged. Experience this creative process and you will never grow old in spirit.

Have you ever known an artist or a dreamer who "retired"?

APPENDIX D

PORTFOLIO

This humble institution is laboratory, skunkworks, studio, and stage, and America's secret weapon in the world's creative wars. Homely, squat, and musty, yes—but also magnificent.

garage

by Erik Calonius

IMAGINE YOURSELF living 100 years ago on Detroit's Bagley Avenue. It's 2 A.M. on June 4, 1896, and the sound of steel striking stone has drawn you out of bed and into the night. The noise and puffs of powdered mortar are coming from the coal shed behind No. 58 Bagley (on the page opposite). Bricks from the outer wall tumble to the ground. Soon you can make out the figure of young Henry Ford and, coming through the door he has just widened with his hammer, a fragile-looking vehicle with four bicycle wheels, a horn made from a doorbell, and a tiller steering wheel. You have just glimpsed Ford's first automobile.

But you have also witnessed the birth of something else just as magical in its way. You have been present at the creation of the American garage. Earlier, there were carriage houses, sheds, barns, privies, and other worthy outbuildings, but the garage as we know it today came with the automobile, a snug place to keep that vulnerable machine out of the weather.

In America, however, the garage is not just a place to protect cars, old magazines, record albums, and toasters that will definitely be repaired someday. It is a laboratory, a skunkworks, a stage, a studio, where dreamers have transformed fantasies into industries that have changed the world. The garage is, in a way, the U.S.'s secret weapon, a partial explanation of why Americans still seem to have an inventive edge. The Japanese have lots of cars but relatively few garages, and cramped ones at that.

In the pages that follow, FORTUNE celebrates a century's worth of these humble domestic laboratories—where Walt Disney drafted his early cartoons; Steve Jobs and Stephen Wozniak pieced together the first personal computer; Lila and DeWitt Wallace nurtured the *Reader's Digest*; Buddy Holly and the Crickets rehearsed the music that helped create rock-and-roll; and C.E. Woolman turned a crop-dusting business into Delta Air Lines. As you read this, thousands of their successors have retreated to their garages, where, between lawn mowers and broken clothes washers, some of them are likely creating the FORTUNE 500 companies of the next century.

REPORTER ASSOCIATE *Shaifali Puri*

Photographs by Diane Cook and Len Jenshel

HENRY FORD GARAGE
58 Bagley Avenue, Detroit

Henry Ford might have passed away in obscurity had it not been for a neighbor who was generous enough not only to give up his rights to a coal shed but to help remodel it to the inventor's convenience as well. In 1896, Ford had been experimenting at home with a primitive gasoline engine, which he placed in the kitchen sink.

150 FORTUNE MARCH 4, 1996

"Garage" by Erik Calonius, *Fortune*, March 4, 1996. Reprinted with permission. To read the full article, visit schusslercreative.com.

Selected Bibliography

Barbour, David. "Dining with Dinosaurs—T-REX Aims to Be the Next Big Thing in Themed Restaurants." *Lighting and Sound America* 3, no. 12 (November 2006): 64–69.

Berman, Lyle, and Marvin Karlins. *I'm All In.* New York: Cardoza Publishing, 2005.

Blumenthal, Ira. *Ready, Blame, Fire.* Glendale, CA: Griffin Publishing Group, 1998.

Boltz Chapman, Mary. "The Age of Dinosaurs—Steven Schussler's T-REX Hopes to Transport Guests to Prehistoric Times." *Chain Leader*, August 2004, 24.

Brodsky, Sascha. "Once Bitten—T-REX Is What's Next for Rainforest Cafe Founder Steven Schussler." *Shopping Centers Today*, June 1, 2005, 33.

Calonius, Erik. "America's Secret Weapon: the Garage." *Fortune*, March 4, 1996, 150–160.

Cason, Luci. "How Schussler Creative Maintains Its 'Wow' Factor—Creativity Is the Engine for Success." *Restaurant Facility Business*, December 2006/January 2007, 14–18.

Cooper, Jonathan. "Red Development Inks Restaurant Partnership Deal." *The Business Journal* (Phoenix, AZ), May 18, 2007.

Elmstrom, Dave. "Will Rainforest Reign? Despite Rapid Growth Plans, One of the Hottest Stocks around Just Might Flourish." *Twin Cities Business Monthly*, January 1998, 32–35.

Ewen, Beth. "Lessons Learned—Three CEOs Tell How They're Building Their Companies." *Upsize Magazine,* June–July 2007, 58–61.

Ewen, Beth. "Rainforest Cafe Founder Rolls out T-REX Chain, Shops Eight More Big Ideas." *Upsize Magazine*, November 2006, 9.

Farkas, David. "Creative Habitat—Steven Schussler's T-REX Is Just the Beginning of the Concepts Coming out of His Idea Lab." *Chain Leader,* July 2006, online exclusive, http://www.chainleader.com.

Fickes, Michael. "All or Nothing at the Rainforest Cafe." *Retail Store Image,* March 1995, 44–51.

Fishman, Susan. "Restaurant Think Tank—Rainforest Cafe Founder Tweaks Seven New Theatrical Food Concepts." *Shopping Center Business*, May 2005, 286.

Fishman, Susan, and Chris Thorn. "Dining with Dinosaurs." *The Midwest's Real Estate Source* 3, no. 9 (May 2005).

Gabler, Ellen. "Rainforest Founder Plots Big Return." *Twin Cities Business Journal*, January 14, 2005, 1.

Gee, David. "Steven Schussler's Themed Restaurants Are Hot, Even in a Cold Economy." *Minnesota Business,* December 2008, 36–41.

Gendron, George. "The Most Original—and Expensive—Business Card in America." *Inc.,* July 1986, 6.

"Great Comebacks: Dogged Pursuit." *Success,* July/August 1987, 35–36.

Heavey, Laurie. "Owner's Mental Attitude Ensures Potential of '50s Club Franchise." *Night Club & Bar*, April 1985, 16–18.

"JukeBox Saturday Night." *Restaurant Business,* July 20, 1985, 134.

Karlins, Marvin. *Romancing the Clock.* 2nd ed. Englewood Cliffs, NJ: Prentice-Hall, 2009.

Krummert, Bob. "Will T-REX Devour K.C.?" *Restaurant Hospitality*, October 2006, 15–16.

Levy, Paul. "The Man Who Makes Things Spin in JukeBox Saturday Night." *Minneapolis Star & Tribune—Sunday Magazine*, February 8, 1987, 6–12.

Marsh, Steve. "Crazy as a Tyrannosaur." *Minneapolis St. Paul*, April, 2006, 105.

McKinney, Matt. "Schussler Has More Themed Attractions in Store." *Minneapolis Star Tribune*, September 29, 2007.

McWilliams, Peter. *You Can't Afford the Luxury of a Negative Thought.* Los Angeles: Prelude Press, 1997.

Mervine, Bob. "Dining with Dinosaurs at Disney—New Themed Restaurant Signals a Makeover for Pleasure Island." *Orlando Business Journal*, March 2006, 61.

Millard, Elizabeth. "Stream of Consciousness." *Minnesota Business*, December 2006, 8.

Navarro, Joe, and Marvin Karlins. *What Every BODY Is Saying.* New York: HarperCollins, 2008.

"New Restaurant Concept Fits Orlando to a T." *Orlando Business Journal*, June 17–23, 2005.

Nodgaard, Lindsey. "Rainforest Café Founder Gives Lecture." *Manitou Messenger*, April 11, 2003, A1.

Norris, Maya. "Road Warrior." *Chain Leader*, January 2007, 54.

Peale, Norman Vincent. *The Power of Positive Thinking.* New York: Fawcett World Library, Crest Book, 1966.

Reilley, Mike. "An Old and New Dining Experience at T-REX." *Orlando Attractions Magazine*, December 2008, 38–41.

Roberts, Rob. "Retail Developers Play Show and Sell." *Kansas City Business Journal* 23, no. 5 (October 15–21, 2004).

Ruggles, Ron. "Concept Innovator Schussler Inks $100M Development Deal." *Nation's Restaurant News,* May 28, 2007, 8.

Sauer, Patrick. "Top of the Food Chain." *Success* 16, no. 8 (November/ December 2006): 69–71.

"Schussler Creative and RED Development for Partnership." *Shopping Center Business,* July 2007.

"Schussler Creative and RED Development Join Forces to Create New Attractions, Themed Restaurants, Hospitality and Shopping Venues." *Forbes,* May 18, 2007.

"Schussler Creative and RED Development to Roll out Eatertainment." *Nation's Restaurant News,* May 18, 2007, Concepts section.

Smith, Joyce, and Mark Wiebe. "Breaking Ground for the Future." *Kansas City Star Newspaper*, October 13, 2004, Business section.

Smith, Ronald J. "JukeBox Sat. Night: Steve Schussler's Dream Come True." *Entrepreneur,* March 1985, 32–36.

Tice, Carol. "Hear Him Roar: Rainforest Cafe Founder's Entrepreneurial Adventures." *Entrepreneur*, February 2007, 20.

"T-REX: An Interview with the Creator—Steve Schussler." *Prehistoric Times* 77 (April/May 2006): 53.

Vomhof, John. "Schussler Creative Plans Multi-Restaurant Rollout." *Minneapolis/St. Paul Business Journal*, May 18, 2007.

About the Author

Steven Schussler, well-known as the creator of **Rainforest Cafe®**, *A Wild Place to Shop and Eat™*, is an innovator with the passion and artistic vision for conceiving concepts that appeal to the masses. Embracing imagination, Steven and his team create restaurants, retail stores, theatrical venues, attractions, and experiences unlike any other! A master at multi-juggling, Steven is The World's Premiere Branding Expert™, Consultant, Entrepreneur, Restaurateur, Teacher, and Motivational Speaker.

Starting his entrepreneurial career early with a paper route at nine years old, Steven reinvented himself many times, with more than a dozen jobs before his sixteenth birthday. As an executive in the television and broadcast industry, he learned to sell intangible concepts. His career in the restaurant industry began with **JukeBox Saturday Night™**, a nostalgic restaurant and nightclub with eight locations nationwide, including Des Moines, IA; Springfield, MA; San Francisco, CA; Minneapolis, MN; and Chicago, IL.

Opening the first Rainforest Cafe location at Mall of America in Bloomington, Minnesota, in October 1994, it became the first restaurant to go public with only one unit open. Steven and his public company built and operated forty-five Rainforest Cafe restaurants in seven years, on three continents, which were sold to Landry's Restaurants in 2000.

In addition to Rainforest Cafe, T-REX, Yak & Yeti, the Boathouse, Hot Dog Hall of Fame, and Green Acres Event Center, Schussler and his creative team continue to develop, market, and build themed restaurants and attractions.

Galaxy Drive In™, *Aliens, Humans and All of Our Four-Legged Friends Welcome™*, located in St. Louis Park, Minnesota, offers an intergalactic, retro-futuristic, and pet-friendly experience with a delicious menu, s'mores kits to roast on fire pits, and oversized outdoor chess and checker sets. All canine visitors receive a free ice cream cone and doggie menu.

Schussler and his creative team have a number of concepts under development. Pictures and descriptions of these can be found at *www.schusslercreative.com/concepts/*

Aerobleu™ *The Spirit of Cool*™

Zi Imperial Kitchen™ Asian *Antiquities and Culinary Art*™

Winter Wonderland™ *The Magic of Winter™ - Eat, Shoppe, Skate & Play™*

Sorcerer's Kitchen™ *School of Wizardry, Food & Magic*™

Musical Garden™ *A Living Work of Art, Food and Music*™

Water, Fire & Ice™ *Polar Ultra Lounge™—The Hottest Place on Ice*™

Pizza Market™ *Italian Kitchen, Wine & Groceria™—The Place to Ciao!*™

St. Tropez, *L'esprit de cool*

Gizmos, Gadgets & Gears, *Great Comfort Foods That America Celebrates*

Dragon World (Schussler Creative has licensed the rights to "Puff the Magic Dragon")

Steven Schussler was honored with the 2017 Eureka! Innovator of the Year Award by *Minneapolis/St. Paul Business Journal* and the 2016 Heritage Preservation Award for his contribution in restoring a historic barn and transforming it to become Green Acres Event Center. He was also named a Pioneer on the "Top 100 People to Know" by *Twin Cities Business* magazine.

Steven Schussler's Rainforest Cafe received forty awards in six years, which include:

- *Fortune* magazine's Top 100 Fastest-Growing Companies in the United States (two consecutive years)
- *Entrepreneur* magazine's Top 100 Entrepreneurs in the Country
- *Nation's Restaurant News*'s Hot Concept Award
- *Orlando Magazine*'s Best Theme Restaurant

Galaxy Drive In, an Intergalactic, Retro-Futuristic Drive-In™—Made on Earth™—Aliens, Humans and All of our Four-Legged Friends Welcome™. A prototype and working laboratory located in St. Louis Park, Minnesota.

- National Retail Federation's National Retailer of the Year
- *Chicago Tribune*'s Best Restaurant for Kids

As a former columnist for *Minnesota Business Journal,* Steven educated readers with new and fascinating stories, advice, and experiences from nationally and internationally recognized business leaders. Steven has also taught an entrepreneurial class for the Carlson School of Business Management at the University of Minnesota.

Schussler donates a portion of his book profits to many different charitable organizations. He has been involved with a variety of organizations, including the Leukemia Society, American Lung Association, Minneapolis Youth Connection, Life Skills Center for Leadership, Special Olympics, Neighborhood House, Animal Humane Society, Caregivers Network, and Smile Network International. Steven Schussler is also a graduate and former copresident of the first graduating class (2007) of the FBI Citizen's Academy, which engages citizens in the process of protecting their communities and country when and if called upon.

As a founding member of Smile Network International, Steven continues to be a lifetime advisor of the board of directors. He is on the board of directors for Kona Grill Inc., which owns and operates twenty-seven upscale casual dining restaurants in seventeen states. Steven is on the community advisory board of the Hennepin County Sheriff's Office. He is also the chairman of the board of Schussler Creative Inc. and an often called-upon consultant to other boards.

INDEX

A

Active listener factor in choosing strategic partners, 235–236
Adaptability, and multitasking, 45
Alcoholic beverages, social responsibility concerning, 193–194
Ambition, 31–34
Amphicars, 69, 89–90, 216–225, 227
"The Artist's Credo" (Bloch), 34
Attention to detail, 45, 59–64, 81
Attractions, as Steve's passion, 13
Awareness, 37
Awareness, maintaining an eye for creative opportunity, 65–70

B

Backfire BBQ, 63–64, 78–80, 88
Bankruptcy and recovery story, 11–12
Barsella, John, 188
Believing in the concept, and getting from no to yes with investors, 127. *See also* Passion
Berman, Lyle
  commitment to invest in Rainforest Cafe, 21
  and Jules Schussler, 182–183
  love of tropical birds, 24
  Lyle's gaming activities in Disney's eyes, 176
  over-budget story, 97–98
  Steven's help with Lyle's casino projects, 160–161
  Steven's persistence with, 25, 26, 122
Big-picture and detail focus, combining, 63
Bisienere, Maribeth, 159
Blake, Laurie, 203–204
Bloch, Douglas, 34
Boathouse Restaurant
  Amphicars, 69, 217–227
  budget overruns, handling, 94–95
  layering at, 48–49
  on the lookout for excellence, 57
  partners in developing, 188
  Shanghai opening, 238
Body language, and making first impressions, 110–111
Book publishing story, 160
Bradford, Keith, 219–221
Bridge burning, avoiding, 181–188
Budgeting, 93–98
Budweiser, 102
Build-A-Bear Workshop, 100–101, 158
Build-A-Dino, 101, 158–159
Business cards, usefulness of, 111–113

C

Card-table concierge job, 66–69, 166
Caring attitude, need for, 147–150
Case, Ron and Kathie, 178–179
Challenge as opportunity, 32–33

Chao, Wing, 220–221
Charitable causes. *See* Philanthropy
Clark, Maxine, 100–101, 158–159
Collaboration factor in choosing strategic partners, 236
Complementary voice factor in choosing strategic partners, 235
Conceive, believe, achieve process, 50–51
Conditional no, working through, 122, 127–128
"Confetti-cash" ticker-tape parade, 86
Contact list, attention to detail, 62–63
Contingency amount to manage cost overruns, 95
Continuous improvement focus, 77–82. *See also* Layering
Creativity
  allowing time for project to evolve, 78–80
  maintaining an eye for opportunity, 65–70
  marketing presentations, 90–91
  multitasking as impetus to, 43

D

Dare, Bud, 176, 177
Deal negotiation, avoiding burning bridges, 186–187
Designated driver (DD) program, 193
Disney, Walt, 144
Disney park marriage proposal scheme, 121
Disney (The Walt Disney Company)
  Amphicar negotiations, 218–221
  appeal of attention to detail to, 61
  becoming a trustworthy partner/vendor for, 176–177
  and Boathouse Restaurant, 94–95, 225–232
  multitasking for T-REX buy-in from, 43–44
  and Rainforest Cafe, 28–29
  Yak & Yeti, 43–44, 81
The Dog House, 187–188
Dreaming, entrepreneurial, 35–39, 43, 48, 144
Dzubnar, Paul, 206–207

E

Earnings
energy expenditure for bigger or smaller dreams, 38
  as themed restaurant commandment, 73
Eden Prairie, Minnesota, 178, 202, 206. *See also* Green Acres Event Center
Education
  failure as education for success, 133–137
  programs as benefit to business, 50
  as themed restaurant commandment, 73
Emphatic vs. conditional no, 127–128

Employees, as themed restaurant commandment, 73
Enhancement opportunities, scanning for, 66–70. *See also* Layering
Ensted, Terry, 207
Entertainment, as themed restaurant commandment, 73
Entrepreneurs
  big-picture vs. detail focus, 63
  the dream of the idea, 35–39
  vs. employed businessperson, 10
  as eternal optimists, 140
  importance of believing in the idea, 51
  sharing successes of other, 159–160
  value of strategic partnerships for, 100, 160–161
Entrepreneur's credo, 259
Environment, as themed restaurant commandment, 73
Environmental conservation projects, 194
Excellence as product goal. *See also* Layering
  and attention to detail, 60–64
  dedication to even when others are at "good enough," 228–229
  "Disney factor" and, 94
  importance of R&D to, 72, 76
  importance of search for, 55–57
  layering, 47–52, 69–70, 80
Experience, importance of creating for customers and investors, 20–24

F

Failure as education for success, 133–137
Feedback during idea development, importance of, 80
Fertitta, Tilman, 184–186
Financial setbacks, working through, 26–27, 135–137, 142–143, 177
First impressions with investors, making good, 108–113
Five senses, as themed restaurant commandment, 73, 76
Flom, Dave, 217, 223
Focus groups to test ideas, 74
Friendships, entrepreneurial, 215–227, 236. *See also* Partnerships
Futurists, entrepreneurs as, 37

G

Gibsons Restaurant Group, 156, 225–226, 235
Going from "no" to "yes"
  Amphicars, 218–221
  Boathouse Restaurant, 225–232
  and choosing strategic partnerships, 235–236
  conditional no, working through, 122, 127–128
  with passion and persistence, 23–24, 26, 122–123, 125–131
Goldfarb, Morris, 88–89
Goodman, John, 161

Graham, Steve, 149
Green Acres Event Center, 61–62, 70, 178, 202–213

H

Hamlin, Don, 9
Handshake, and first impressions, 109–110
"Helicopter view" of entrepreneur, 63
Hightop Hospitality, 206–207
Hilton, Conrad, 60
Honesty and building trust, 176–179
Hospitality industry, passion to please as integral to, 16
Hughes, Langston, 38–39
Humility in the face of failure, 136

I

Iacocca, Lee, 161
Iger, Bob, 238
Integrity factor in choosing strategic partners, 235
Investors
  Berman as investor, 21, 25, 26, 97–98, 122
  creating an experience for, 20–24
  Fertitta as investor, 185–186
  handling budget issues with, 94–97
  importance of generating trust, 176
  mutually supportive network with entrepreneurs, 160–161
  selling yourself as well as your idea to, 106–113
  using five-senses experience to convince, 76
  value of attention to detail for attracting, 64
Irvine, Robert, 222

J

John, Sharon Price, 101
Juke Box Saturday Night
  budget vs. excellence, 97
  flirting with failure at, 136
  free rides home for customers, 193–194
  getting to know the area for a new venue, 153
  honesty with Disney's difficult questions about, 176–177
  marketing for, 84, 85, 112
  perception management, 165–166
  rocky start as retail shop, 11–14
  strategic partnerships, 102–103

K

Kansas City, bringing T-REX to, 72, 88, 149, 154
Katzenberg, Jeffrey, 238
Kazeminy, Nasser, 161

L

Labor of love, entrepreneurial mission as, 201–211
Landry's Restaurants Inc., 24, 96, 184–185

Layering, and improving quality of experience, 47–52, 69–70, 80
Leadership, passion's importance in, 16
Leaving something for people to remember you by, 111–112
LeBoeuf, Michael, 156
Life balance factor in choosing strategic partners, 236
Lincoln, Abraham, 118
Listening carefully, art of, 110–111
Lombardo, Steve III, 188
Lombardo, Steve Sr., 188, 225, 235
Loving your work, importance of, 17–18. *See also* Passion
Lowe, Dan, 149

M

MacKay, Harvey, 101–102, 160
Making people feel special, 151–156
Maples, Marla, 123
Marketing, 83–92
  and ambition, 33–34
  Amphicars and turning negative to positive, 89–90
  attention to detail in, 63–64
  Backfire BBQ motorcycling entrance, 88
  being willing to go to the customer to pitch, 90–91
  creative presentations, 90–91
  currency confetti parade, 85–87
  education and, 50
  "Homer Hanky" cleaning service, 85
  importance of visibility in selling product, 84–85
  for Juke Box Saturday Night, 84, 85, 112
  post-marketing improvements to product or service, 81–82
  reacting quickly to publicity opportunities, 89
  T-REX opening in Kansas City, 88
  value of multitasking for, 43–45
Marketing yourself, 105–113, 128–131, 170
Mashal, Fouad, 155–156
McWilliams, Peter, 196
Media contacts and positive publicity, 169–173
Minnesota Twins, 85–87
Mission statement, Schussler Creative Inc., 257
Multitasking as entrepreneurial gift, 41–45, 49
Murray, Bill, 160
Music, as themed restaurant commandment, 73
Myslajek, Tim, 142–143, 250

N

Navarro, Joe, 110

O

Opportunity awareness, 65–70
Optimism, power of, 18–19, 37, 139–144
Orange County Choppers, 79–80
"Oyster Girl" figure, 229

P

Palazzo, Gloria, 240
Parties as great public relations, 172–173
Partnerships, cultivating business, 85, 99–103, 160–161, 233–238
Passion, 15–29
  and ambition, 33–34
  Boathouse Restaurant, 219–227
  build it and they will come philosophy, 18–21
  and the dream, 36
  in going from "no" to "yes," 127
  Green Acres Event Center, 210
  and keeping a lookout for opportunity builders, 69
  marketing, 88
  and persistence, 26–27
  Rainforest Cafe concept, 21–27
  and R&D, 74
  and selling yourself to investors, 107
  taking risks to follow, 11–12
  as themed restaurant commandment, 73
Peale, Norman Vincent, 50
People, 145–188. *See also* Investors; Partnerships
  avoiding bridge burning, 181–188
  caring attitude, 147–150
  friend or foe mindset when working with, 215, 226
  friendships, 215–227, 236
  giving people second chances, 181–188
  making people feel special, 151–156
  media contacts and positive publicity, 169–173
  perception management, 163–167
  supporting others in achieving their goals, 157–161
  trust, power of, 175–179
Perception management, 163–167
Persist-and-prevail philosophy, 118–119, 122, 202–211
Persistence, 115–144
  and entrepreneurial mission as labor of love, 201–211
  failure as education to success, 133–137
  going from "no" to "yes," 23–24, 26, 122–123, 125–131
  meeting failure with, 133–137
  and optimism, 139–144
  as path to success, 117–124
Personality, 1–52
  ambition, 31–34
  dreaming, 35–39, 43, 48, 144
  layer management, 47–52, 69–70, 80
  multitasker, 41–45, 49
  passionate, 15–29
  risk-taking, 3–14
PETA, 164–165
Peterson, Karen, 188
Philanthropy, 185, 189–198
Physical appearance, and first impressions, 109
Portillo, Dick, 187–188
Portillo, Sharon, 188
Portillo's Hot Dogs, 187–188

Prioritizing, multitasking with attention to detail, 45
Product, 53–113. *See also* Marketing
  attention to detail, 45, 59–64, 81
  being on the lookout for new opportunities, 65–70
  budgeting, 93–98
  continuous improvement focus, 77–82
  excellence as goal, 55–57
  layering to improve, 47–52, 69–70, 80
  marketing yourself in marketing your, 105–113, 128–131, 170
  research and development, 9, 69, 71–76, 221, 223, 231–232
  strategic partnerships, 85, 99–103, 160–161, 233–238
Public relations
  creating positive press, 169–173
  handling negative publicity, 89–90
  publicity stunts, effectiveness of, 85–89

R

Rainforest Cafe
  budget overrun at Mall of America, 97–98
  challenges of, 140–141, 142
  hiring homeless at, 192–193
  and Jules Schussler, 183–184
  layering in, 49–50, 80
  loss of live birds, 50, 95–96
  original concept and prototype, 19–28
  PETA protest handling, 164–165
  sale to Landry's, 184–185
Relationships in business. *See* Investors; People
Research and development, 9, 69, 71–76, 221, 223, 231–232
Retail component, 13, 100–101, 228–232
Return on innovation, 73
Ridgeway, Paul, 85–86
Risk-taking, 3–14, 76
Rittenberg, Jimmy, 12–13, 97
Rodeo Nightclub, 12
Royal Crown Cola, 102, 103
Rubber ducks issue for Boathouse retail, 229–232
Ryan-Schussler, Sunhi, 205, 209

S

Schussler, Jason, 240
Schussler, John, 240
Schussler, Jules, 182–184, 240
Schussler, Robert, 240
Second chances, wisdom in giving, 181–188
Selling yourself, importance of, 105–113, 128–131, 170
September 11, 2001 terrorist attack, 91
Shane, Larry, 188, 225
Shane, Steve, 225
Ship job hunting stunt, 120
Siegel, David, 91
Silver Gull Beach Club, 66–69, 166
Simon Property Group, 90–91
Skees, Theron, 223

Smile Network International, 196–197, 198
Social responsibility, 185, 189–198
Sporting events, enhancing publicity around, 85–86
Strategic partnerships, cultivating, 85, 99–103, 160–161, 233–238
Sullivan, Patty, 188
Superbowl Sunday 2018, 88–89
Superman job hunting stunt, 5–9, 119–120
Supporting others in achieving their goals, 157–161

T

Teutel, Paul Sr., 79
Themed restaurants. See also *individual restaurants by name*
  11 Commandments, 72–73
  quest for excellence, 56
  as Steve's passion, 13
T-REX
  Build-A-Dino, 158–159
  challenges of, 141–142, 143
  creative marketing for, 88, 90–91
  desert trip inspiration for, 36
  initial Kansas City project, 72, 149, 154
  listening and flexibility in making improvements, 80
  multitasking for Disney's buy-in, 43–44
  perception management, 166–167
  power of persistence in developing, 122–123
  relationship story, 149
  research and development, 74–75
  retail component, 100–101
  value of building relationships, 154
Trump, Donald, 123
Trust, power of, 175–179
TV advertising, selling of, 128–130

U

Unionization effort, and managing perceptions, 165

V

Valentini, David, 152–153
Valentini, Kim, 196–197, 198
Voicemail and hold messaging, 113, 171–172
Volunteering, value of, 196, 198

W

Websites, as public relations tools, 172
Winter Wonderland, 61
Wintle, Walter D., 51–52
Work-life balance, 236–237

Y

Yak & Yeti, 43–44, 81

Z

Zappia, Tom, 202–203